C. R. Lavey
1462 Cambridge Rd
Lansing Mich 48910

D1175065

GREGG SHORTHAND DICTIONARY

By

JOHN ROBERT GREGG, S.C.D.

Anniversary Edition

GREGG PUBLISHING DIVISION

McGraw-Hill Book Company, Inc.

New York Chicago San Francisco Dallas Toronto London

GREGG SHORTHAND DICTIONARY

ANNIVERSARY EDITION

Shorthand Plates Written by
WINIFRED KENNA RICHMOND

PUBLISHED BY GREGG PUBLISHING DIVISION

McGraw-Hill Book Company, Inc.

Printed in the United States of America

PREFACE

The preparation of the Anniversary Edition of the Gregg Shorthand Manual was a big undertaking. When it was finished, there remained tasks almost as great in the revision of "Progressive Exercises," "Gregg Speed Studies," and the keys to all these books. These done, we were obliged to revise all of the supplementary books in harmony with the changes that had been made. It is with a sigh of relief that we put the finishing touches on this Dictionary, which practically completes the series.

In the revision of all the basic texts, we were not content with changing the forms for words affected by the changes in the Anniversary Edition, or with substituting new exercises in accordance with the new arrangement of the rules and material, because we wanted to give effect to many improvements suggested by our study and experience with the old editions, or which were suggested by our many teacher friends. All the books incorporate new ideas, new material, new methods.

Now as to this Dictionary: The new features are fully set forth in the Introduction—features that I believe will render the book much more valuable than any previous edition.

In sending it forth, I desire to acknowledge my indebtedness to Mr. Rupert P. SoRelle and Mr. Louis A. Leslie for their assistance in compiling the lists of words used, and in classifying them in the manner set forth in the Introduction. Special credit should be given Mrs. Winifred Kenna Richmond for the artistic manner in which she has written the shorthand forms.

JOHN ROBERT GREGG.

INTRODUCTION

A dictionary is primarily a reference book. A good dictionary, however, properly used, should be far more than that. This is particularly true of a shorthand dictionary, which should be a guide so clear that a beginner can readily locate the shorthand outline for any given word, but which at the same time should possess all the resources needed to satisfy the most advanced writer, whether a teacher or a court reporter.

The Gregg Shorthand Dictionary should not only teach the beginner, but should help the expert to crystallize his knowledge by careful classification of the shorthand forms and consistency in the use of abbreviating devices.

In the present dictionary, we have endeavored to do these things. In this brief Introduction we shall state some of the principles followed in obtaining consistency of outline. These rules cover the treatment of some frequent sound combinations, and a thorough acquaintance with them will often make it unnecessary to refer to the word list itself for an outline.

One of the most fascinating features of Gregg Shorthand is the manner in which the principle of analogy is applied. Nothing is more helpful to the shorthand writer than this principle properly used. In effect, it means that, once you have learned the forms for one or more words of any classification, you may then write any similar word ending in the same way. For example, when you know the shorthand forms for *agitate* and *hesitate,* and therefore know that the ending *tate* is expressed by *ta,* you can write any similar words, such as *dictate* or *imitate.*

In other words, the material given in this Introduction is not to be memorized, but is to be studied intelligently in order that you may see the underlying principles governing the formation of the outlines. Nothing is arbitrary —there is always a *reason why,* even though at first sight it may not be apparent.

First, we should explain that the following have been eliminated as being unnecessary:

1. Short, simple words that any student who is still working on the early part of the Manual can easily write, such words as *cat, dog*, etc.

2. Purely "dictionary words." Every word in the list of nearly 19,000 is a word in good usage. If any of the words seem unfamiliar to you, however, look them up in an ordinary English dictionary and jot down the definition in your shorthand dictionary.

3. Certain derivatives that are formed in accordance with the rules given in the textbook, such as the numerous derivatives of the suffix *ulate*, and some others. In order to save space and make room for more root words, a complete table of these suffix derivatives is given in this Introduction. In case there should be doubt as to the correct writing of one of the derivatives, reference to this table will make the matter clear.

The Gregg Shorthand Dictionary contains the following indispensable features:

1. A list of the 19,000 most frequently used words in the English language. The words for which the shorthand forms are immediately obvious have been omitted.

2. Many past tenses, plurals, and other derivative forms that were not included in previous editions of the shorthand dictionary.

3. Derivatives in every case grouped under the root word in easily accessible form. Since the root words in type project slightly beyond the margin of the type column, the finding of any word is greatly facilitated—it is necessary only to look down the comparatively small list of root words that stand out at the left of each column.

4. Direct derivatives, and in some cases closely allied words, are listed under their root words. This has been done in order to emphasize the value of the analogical building of outlines, and also in the belief that the practice of a group of related outlines is more valuable than the practice of the isolated outlines.

FOUR FREQUENTLY USED DERIVATIVES

The four derivatives most frequently formed are the past tense, the plural, the negative, and the comparative and superlative degrees of adjectives.

THE PAST TENSE. It may be helpful to summarize and condense the rules given in the Manual for the formation of the past tense.

1. After abbreviated words, a disjoined *t* is placed close to the preceding character to express the past tense. This includes:

    a. Brief forms, as in *changed*.

    b. Words written in accordance with the abbreviating principle, as in *established*.

    c. Words written with a suffix, as in *insulted*.

    d. Words in which the last letter of the primitive form is omitted, as in *demanded*.

2. A disjoined *t* is used to express the past tense after words written in full when the joining of the *t* or *d* would not give a distinctive or facile outline, as in *fancied, glared, neared*.

3. The past tense is expressed by joined *t* or *d*:

    a. After words written in full, as in *printed, checked*, except in the few cases coming under the preceding paragraph.

    b. In derivatives ending in *ct*, as in *contracted*.

    c. In verbs ending in *l*, the special method described in paragraph 136 in the Manual is used, as in *killed*.

    d. After suffixes that give a facile and legible joining, as in *mentioned, stipulated*.

    e. After many brief forms containing the last character of the word, as in *asked, charged, worked*.

PLURALS. The formation of plurals is clearly explained in paragraphs 55, 74, and 83 in the Manual.

NEGATIVE FORMS. The vowel is omitted in the prefixes *en, in, un, em, im, um* when the prefix is followed by a consonant, as in *unseen, impossible, unmask, uninvited, unimportant*.

When a vowel follows a prefix, the initial vowel is written, as in *uneasy*, unless the vowel that follows belongs to another prefix or to a brief form, in which case it is not necessary to insert the vowel in the negative prefix, as in *inexpensive, unorganized*.

Negative words beginning with *un* or *im* in which the *n* or *m* is doubled are distinguished from the positive forms by omitting one of the doubled consonants and inserting the initial vowel, as in *unknown, immodest*.

COMPARATIVE AND SUPERLATIVE FORMS. The comparative form of an adjective is usually written by simply joining an *r* to the primitive form, as in *quicker, slower.* If, however, the adjective is written in full and ends in a straight line, the reversing principle is used for the comparative form, as in *larger, later;* when a brief form ends with the last consonant of a word, the reversed circle is used to make the comparative form after straight lines, as in *sooner, stranger;* after brief forms, abbreviated words, and words ending in a reversed circle, a disjoined *r* is used, as in *worker, purer, nearer,* unless the joined form is distinctive, in which case it may be used, as in *smaller, greater.*

The termination *est* is expressed by *es* in words ending in a consonant when the word is written in full, as in *cheapest, broadest.* This rule also applies to brief forms or contractions when the final consonant of the shorthand form is also the final consonant of the word, as in *soonest, strangest.*

The termination *est* is usually expressed by a disjoined *st* after brief forms, abbreviated words, or words ending in a vowel, as in *stillest, busiest,* but the *st* may be joined when a distinctive form is obtained, as in *fullest, truest.*

FORMATION OF ADVERBS. Adverbs formed by the addition of *ly* to the adjective are written in shorthand by adding the small circle, signifying *ly,* to the primitive form of the adjective. The only exceptions to this rule are *friendly, immediately, thoroughly, respectfully.*

THE ENDING TION

So many words end with the suffix *tion,* in its various spellings, that in forming derivatives a shorthand outline is considered to end with the final letter of a word if the word ends with the suffix *tion.* By so doing, that great class of words may be written in accordance with such rules as those in paragraphs 76 and 59 (2) of the Anniversary Manual.

Words ending in *tionist* are written with the joined *es,* as in *abolitionist, evolutionist, elocutionist.* So, also, we are able to use the reversed circle for such forms as, *auctioneer, stationer, executioner,* and the joined *d* for forms like *mentioned, commissioned, old fashioned.*

Other examples showing the manner in which the outlines ending in *tion, sion, cien* may be regarded as written in full are such classes of words as *professional, national, provisional, sensational, rational; efficient, deficient, proficient; efficiency, deficiency, proficiency.*

THE ENDING ATE

T is omitted in the terminations *rate, late, tate.* The *t* is written in the terminations *fate, vate, mate, nate.* The *at* is omitted in the terminations *cate, gate.* The following brief list of examples will make this clear:

-rate
accurate, commemorate, confederate, decorate, liberate, narrate, obdurate, operate, penetrate, perpetrate, venerate, vibrate. (In a few words the abbreviating principle is applied: *coöperate, elaborate, inaugurate, recuperate, refrigerate, separate.* To form derivatives add *s* for *-rates,* a disjoined *v* for *-rative,* a disjoined *r* for *-rator.*)

-late
annihilate, desolate, dilate, disconsolate, inflate, isolate, mutilate, oscillate, scintillate, translate, violate, ventilate.

-tate
agitate, annotate, devastate, dictate, facilitate, felicitate, gravitate, hesitate, imitate, irritate, necessitate, rotate, vegetate. (Except *meditate.*)

-fate,
-vate
phosphate, aggravate, captivate, cultivate, elevate, excavate, renovate.

-mate
animate, chromate, consummate, cremate, estimate, intimate, sublimate, ultimate, primate.

-nate
alienate, alternate, assassinate, coördinate, dominate, eliminate, fascinate, illuminate, incriminate, indeterminate, inordinate, nominate, originate, predominate, subordinate, terminate, unfortunate. (In the terminations given above, the *t* is retained when a double vowel precedes, as in *affiliate, alleviate, appropriate, conciliate, create, delineate, humiliate, radiate,* except *retaliate, appreciate, enunciate.*)

-cate
abdicate, adjudicate, complicate, confiscate, delicate, deprecate, eradicate, fabricate, implicate, indicate, intricate, locate, allocate, dislocate, lubricate, medicate, suffocate, syndicate, vindicate. (Write *ksh* for *-cation* in words so abbreviated. There are special abbreviations for *certificate, duplicate, communicate, prevaricate, reciprocate, educate.* We write in full for the sake of greater legibility the words *vacate, desiccate, dedicate, predicate, extricate, advocate.*)

-gate
abrogate, aggregate, castigate, congregate, conjugate, corrugate, instigate, interrogate, investigate, irrigate, litigate, mitigate, navigate, obligate, propagate, relegate, segregate, subjugate, surrogate, variegate. (Write *gsh* for *-gation* in words so abbreviated. The abbreviating principle is applied to *delegate, promulgate.* We write in full *legate, frigate.*)

MODIFICATION OF WORD FORMS

In forming compound words, it is often necessary to change somewhat the form of one of the words. Examples of this are: *cobweb, featherweight, flywheel, footwear, neckwear, hoodwink, horsewhip, lukewarm, milkweed, whirlwind.*

FREQUENTLY RECURRING SYLLABLES

The principle of analogy is of the greatest value to the writer of a system in which it may be used to its fullest extent, as is the case with Gregg Shorthand. We shall point out here some of the useful analogical forms that are not given as such in the Manual; many of them fall under the abbreviating principle. In order to conserve space, the shorthand forms are not given, as they may easily be ascertained from the word list of this dictionary. Knowing the outline for any one of the words, and knowing that all similar combinations are written analogically, it will be a simple matter to construct the outlines for yourself. The lists are given for convenience in practice and so that you may study the application of the principle:

-ish   abolish, banish, blemish, brutish, burnish, cherish, childish, famish, finish, flourish, foolish, furnish, girlish, nourish, perish, polish, punish, relish, Spanish, stylish, tarnish, vanish, varnish.

-let   booklet, bracelet, circlet, coverlet, eyelet, gauntlet, gimlet, goblet, inlet, outlet, ringlet, streamlet, tablet, violet. (The ending *ette* is written in full, as in *palette, roulette, silhouette.*)

-cious   (All but a few words with this ending may be written under the abbreviating principle without the *us.*) audacious, atrocious, avaricious, capacious, delicious, efficacious, facetious, fallacious, ferocious, fictitious, loquacious, malicious, meretricious, ostentatious, pernicious, precocious, propitious, sagacious, spacious, superstitious, tenacious, veracious, vivacious, voracious. (In some words having the *cious* ending, it is advisable to add the *us* in order to secure a more legible outline. This is usually true of words having a similar form in *tion*, as in *captious, cautious, infectious, suspicious, vexatious, vicious.*)

-fuse   confuse, diffuse, infuse, profuse, refuse, transfuse.

-nction   compunction, conjunction, disjunction, function, injunction, junction, sanction.

-mand   command, countermand, demand, reprimand.

-ive   arrive, deprive, derive, revive, survive.

-meter   barometer, chronometer, speedometer, thermometer, diameter.

-pel   compel, dispel, expel, impel, propel, repel, spell. (The past tense of all the words ending in *pel* is formed by raising the end of the *l* to show the addition of *d*. Most of them form a derivative in *pulsion,* which is indicated by the addition of *tion* to the primitive form.)

-volve   devolve, evolve, involve, revolve. (Cf. *absolve, dissolve, resolve.*)

-tain   attain, ascertain, captain, certain, contain, detain, entertain, fountain, maintain, mountain, obtain, pertain, sustain.

-uate   accentuate, actuate, attenuate, effectuate, extenuate, graduate, insinuate, perpetuate. (All these words form derivatives in *tion*.)

-ject   abject, deject, eject, inject, project, reject.

-tern,   cistern, eastern, lantern, modern, nocturne, pattern, subaltern,
-dern   western.

-gent,   contingent, diligent, divergent, emergent, exigent, indigent, indul-
-gence   gent, intelligent, negligent. (All these words form a derivative in *gence,* and some in *gency*.)

-port   comport, deport, disport, export, import, passport, purport, sport.

-verse,   diverse, diversity, diversion, diverge; converse, conversion, con-
-versity,   verge; perverse, perversity, perversion; adverse, adversity; inverse,
-version,   inversion; reverse, reversion; subversion; obverse; university. (*Uni-*
-verge   *verse* is written under the abbreviating principle.)

-titude   altitude, aptitude, certitude, fortitude, latitude, platitude. (Except *gratitude.*)

-ric   bishopric, cambric, choleric, fabric, gastric, lyric, metric, theatric.

-vity   brevity, levity, nativity, passivity, captivity, activity, gravity, productivity.

-ntic   romantic, pedantic, Atlantic, authentic.

-ngle   angle, bangle, bungle, entangle, disentangle, mingle, mangle, surcingle, tangle, tingle, wrangle. (The *l* is omitted from the word *single* as the word occurs so frequently. The *l* is also omitted from such derivatives of *angle* as *rectangle, triangle, quadrangle.*)

-ular   angular, cellular, jugular, muscular, nebular, ocular, oracular, secular, tabular, titular, tubular, vehicular. (We may take advantage of the abbreviating principle, however, in *binocular, molecular, spectacular, vernacular; singular, rectangular, triangular.*)

-arious   gregarious, multifarious, nefarious, precarious, vicarious.

-uous   arduous, assiduous, contemptuous, continuous, deciduous, fatuous,

incongruous, ingenuous, impetuous, presumptuous, sinuous, strenuous, sumptuous, tempestuous, tortuous, unctuous, virtuous.

-eous beauteous, bounteous, courteous, cutaneous, duteous, erroneous, extraneous, hideous, igneous, piteous, plenteous.

-tial, artificial, beneficial, circumstantial, commercial, credential, essen-
-cial tial, influential, initial, judicial, martial, partial, penitential, pestilential, providential, provincial, prudential, residential, social, substantial, superficial.

DERIVATIVES OF COMMON ENDINGS

In the following list of the derivative forms of the suffixes and common endings of words, one complete set of derivatives is given in each case. From the outlines on the next page, any similar words may be constructed:

-scribe describe, describes, described, description, descriptive, describable, subscriber.

-pose dispose, disposes, disposed, disposition, disposable.

-pute dispute, disputes, disputed, disputation, disputable, disputant.

-spect prospect, prospects, prospected, inspection, prospective, prospector.

-quire acquire, acquires, acquired, acquisition, acquirement.

-pire aspire, aspires, aspired, aspiration, aspirant.

-city capacity, capacities.

-sure measure, measures, measured, measurable, measurement, measureless.

-flect reflect, reflects, reflected, reflection, reflective, reflector.

-sult consult, consults, consulted, consultation, consultative, consultant.

-tic critic, critics, critical, critically.

-ulate emulate, emulates, emulated, emulation, emulative, emulator, emulatory, postulant, immaculately.

-logy psychology, psychologic, psychological, psychologically, psychologist, psychologists, psychologize, theologian.

-ograph photograph, photographs, photographed, photography, photographer, photographic, photographical, photographically.

-egraph telegraph, telegraphs, telegraphed, telegraphy, telegrapher, telegraphical, telegraphically.

-stic domestic, domestics, domesticate, domesticates, domesticated, domestication, domestically.

DERIVATIVES OF COMMON ENDINGS

-scribe

-pose

-pute

-spect

-quire

-pire   -city

-sure

-flect

-sult

-tic   -ulate

-logy

-ograph

-egraph

-stic

GREGG SHORTHAND DICTIONARY

A

aback

abaft

abandon

abandonment

abate

abatable

abated

abatement

unabated

abbot

abbreviate

abbreviation

unabbreviated

abdicate

abdicated

abdication

abdomen

abdominal

abduct

abduction

abed

aberrance

aberrant

aberration

abet

abeyance

abhor

abhorrence

abhorrent

abide

abjure

abjuration

abjures

ablative

able

ability

able-bodied

ably

disability

disable

enable

inability

unable

ablution

abnegation

abnormal

abnormality

abnormity

aboard

abolish

abolition

abolitionist

abominate

abominable

abomination

aboriginal

aborigines

abound

about

whereabouts	absolute	abuses
above	absolutely	abusive
abrade	absolution	disabuse
abrasion	absolutism	abut
abrasive	absolve	abutment
unabraded	absorb	abutter
abreast	absorbed	abyss
abridge	absorbent	abysmal
abridgment	absorption	acacia
unabridged	abstain	academy
abrogate	abstainer	academic
abrogated	abstemious	academician
abrogation	abstinence	accede
abrupt	abstinent	accelerate
abruptly	abstract	acceleration
abruptness	abstractedly	accelerator
abscess	abstraction	accent
abscond	abstruse	accentuate
absconder	absurd	accentuation
absence	absurdity	unaccented
absent	abundance	accept
absentee	abundant	acceptability
absently	superabundant	acceptable
absent-mindedly	abuse	acceptance
absinth	abused	acceptation

accepts

non-acceptance

unacceptable

access

accessibility

accessible

accession

accessory

inaccessible

accidence

accident

accidental

accidents

acclaim

acclaimed

acclamation

acclimate

acclimatize

accolade

accommodate

accommodation

unaccommodating

accompany

accompaniment

accompanist

unaccompanied

accomplice

complicity

accomplish

accomplishment

accord

accordance

accordingly

accordion

accost

accosted

account

accountable

accountancy

accountant

unaccountable

accredit

accretion

accrue

accrual

accumulate

accurate

accuracy

accurately

inaccuracy

inaccurately

accuse

accusation

accusative

accustom

unaccustomed

acerbity

acetate

acetic

acetylene

achievement

achromatic

acid

acidity

acidulate

acidulous

acknowledge

acknowledges

acknowledgment

acolyte

aconite

acorn

acoustic

acquaint

acquaintance

acquaintances	active	adamantine
unacquainted	activity	adapt
acquiesce	actor	adaptability
acquiescence	actress	adaptable
acquiescent	acts	adaptation
acquire	enact	adapter
acquired	inactive	adaptive
acquirement	inactivity	addendum
acquires	react	addenda
acquisition	reactionary	adder
acquisitive	reenact	addict
acquittal	transact	addiction
acrid	actual	addition
acridity	actuality	additional
acrimonious	actually	additionally
acrimony	actuary	address
acrobat	actuate	addresses
acrobatic	actuated	addressograph
acropolis	acute	readdressed
across	acuity	self-addressed
acrostic	acumen	unaddressed
act	acuteness	adduce
acted	adage	adduces
action	adagio	adenoid
actionable	adamant	adept

adequate
adequacy
adequately
inadequate
adhere
adhered
adherence
adherent
adheres
adhesion
adhesive
adieu
adjacent
adjective
adjoin
adjoined
adjourn
adjourned
adjudge
adjudicate
adjudication
adjudicator
adjunct
adjure
adjures

adjust
adjustable
adjuster
readjust
unadjusted
adjutant
administer
administration
administrative
administrator
administratrix
admirable
admiral
admiralty
admiration
admire
admirer
admires
admissible
admissibility
admission
inadmissible
admit
admittance
admitted

admixture
admonish
admonition
admonitory
adobe
adolescence
adolescent
adopt
adoption
adoptive
adore
adorable
adoration
adorn
adornment
unadorned
adroit
adsorption
adulation
adult
adulterate
adulteration
unadulterated
adumbration
ad valorem

advance
advanced
advancement
advances
advantage
advantageous
advantages
disadvantage
advent
adventitious
adventure
adventurer
adventuresome
adventurous
adverb
adverbial
adverse
adversary
adversity
advert
advertise
advertisement
advertiser
advice
advisability

advisable
advised
adviser
advises
advisory
inadvisable
advocate
advocacy
adz
Aeolian
aeon
aerate
aerial
aerify
aesthetic
aesthetics
affable
affability
affect
affectation
affectionate
disaffected
unaffectedly
affiance
affidavit

affiliate
affiliated
affiliation
affinity
affirm
affirmation
affirmative
disaffirm
affix
afflatus
afflict
affliction
affluence
afford
afforded
affright
affront
effrontery
aforementioned
aforesaid
afraid
unafraid
after
afterclap
after-dinner

aftermath	agile	air-tight
afternoon	agility	airway
afterthought	agitate	alabaster
afterwards	agitated	alacrity
again	agitation	alarm
against	agitator	albatross
ageless	agnostic	albino
agent	agnosticism	album
agency	agony	albumen
reagent	agonize	alchemist
agglomeration	agrarian	alcohol
agglutination	agree	alcoholic
aggrandize	agreeability	alcoholism
aggrandizement	agreeable	non-alcoholic
aggravate	agreed	alcove
aggravated	agreement	alderman
aggravation	disagreeable	alert
aggregate	agriculture	algebra
aggregation	agricultural	algebraic
aggress	agronomy	alibi
aggression	aground	alien
aggressive	ague	alienable
aggressor	ailanthus	alienate
aggrieved	aileron	alienist
aghast	airily	inalienable

alike		allure		altogether	
alimentary		alluvial		altruism	
alimony		almanac		altruistic	
aliquot		almighty		alum	
alive		almond		aluminum	
alkali		almost		alumnus	
alkaline		alms		alumni	
alkaloid		aloud		always	
allegation		alphabet		amalgam	
allegiance		alphabetic		amalgamate	
alleviate		alphabetical		amalgamation	
alleviation		already		amanuensis	
alliance		also		amaranth	
alligator		altar		amateur	
alliteration		alter		amatory	
allocate		alterable		amazed	
allocution		alteration		amazement	
allopathy		unalterable		ambassador	
allotment		altercation		ambassadorial	
allow		alternate		amber	
allowable		alternation		ambidextrous	
allowance		alternative		ambient	
disallow		alternator		ambiguous	
allude		although		ambiguity	
allusion		altitude		ambition	

ambitious	amnesty	anagram
amble	among	analogy
ambrosia	amongst	analogous
ambrosial	amorous	analyze
ambulance	amortize	analysis
ambuscade	amortization	analyst
ambush	amount	analytical
ameliorate	amounted	angel
amelioration	amperage	angelic
amenable	amphibious	archangel
amend	amphibian	anger
amendment	ample	angrily
amenity	amplification	angle
American	amplifier	quadrangle
un-American	amplitude	rectangle
amethyst	amputate	triangle
amiable	amputation	Anglo-Saxon
amiability	amuse	anguish
amicable	amuses	angular
amity	anachronism	angularity
unamiable	anachronistic	aniline
amidships	anaconda	animadversion
ammonia	anaemia	animal
ammunition	anaesthesia	animate
amnesia	anaesthetic	animated

animation	annoyance	antagonist
inanimate	annoyed	antagonistic
reanimate	annual	antecedent
animus	annually	antechamber
animosity	annuals	antedate
ankle	annuity	antediluvian
annals	perennial	antelope
annalist	semiannual	antenna
annexation	superannuate	antepenult
annihilate	annular	anterior
annihilation	anodyne	anteroom
anniversary	anoint	anthology
anno Domini	anomaly	anthracite
annotate	anomalous	anthrax
annotation	anonymous	anthropoid
announce	anonymity	anthropology
announced	another	antic
announcement	answer	anticipate
announcer	answerable	anticipation
annunciation	answered	anticipatory
annunciator	answers	unanticipated
denounce	unanswerable	anticlimax
pronounce	ant	antidote
unannounced	antagonize	antilogy
annoy	antagonism	antimony

antipathy	apartment	apothegm
antiphonal	compartment	apotheosis
antipodes	department	appanage
antique	apathy	apparatus
antiquarian	apathetic	apparatuses
antiquary	aperture	apparel
antiquated	apex	appeal
antiquity	aphasia	appellant
antisepsis	aphorism	appellate
antiseptic	apiary	appear
antithesis	apocalypse	apparent
antitoxin	apocope	apparition
antler	apocrypha	appearance
antonym	apogee	disappear
anvil	apology	appeasable
anxious	apologetic	unappeasable
anxiety	apologies	append
any	apologist	appendage
anyhow	apologize	appendix
anyone	apoplexy	appendicitis
anything	apostasy	apperceive
anyway	apostolic	apperception
anywhere	apostrophe	appertain
aorta	apostrophize	appurtenance
apart	apothecary	appurtenant

appetite	depreciate	apricot
appetizing	apprehend	apropos
apply	apprehended	apt
appliance	apprehension	aptitude
applicability	apprehensive	aptly
applicable	misapprehension	aqueous
applicant	apprentice	aquarium
application	apprenticeship	aquatic
applied	approach	aqueduct
appoint	approachable	aquiline
appointee	unapproachable	arabesque
appointees	approbation	arable
appointive	appropriate	arbiter
appointment	appropriately	arbitrage
disappoint	appropriateness	arbitrament
reappoint	appropriation	arbitrary
apportion	inappropriate	arbitrate
reapportionment	misappropriate	arbitration
apposite	unappropriated	arbitrator
apposition	approve	arboreal
appraisal	approval	arbutus
appreciate	approved	arcade
appreciable	disapproved	archaic
appreciation	approximate	archangel
appreciative	approximation	archbishop

archduchy	arithmetical	arranges
archeology	arm	derange
archer	armament	disarrange
archery	armature	rearrange
archipelago	armchair	unarranged
architect	armful	arrest
architectural	armistice	arrive
archives	armor	arrival
arctic	armorer	arrived
antarctic	armorial	arrogance
ardor	armory	arrogant
ardent	armpit	arsenal
arduous	disarmed	arsenic
argon	forearmed	arson
Argonaut	unarmed	art
argue	Armenian	artful
argument	arnica	artfulness
argumentation	aroma	artless
argumentative	aromatic	artlessness
arid	arouse	artery
aridity	aroused	arterial
aristocrat	arpeggio	arteriosclerosis
aristocracy	arraignment	arthritis
aristocratic	arrange	artichoke
arithmetic	arrangement	article

articulate	ascetic	aspire
disarticulate	asceticism	aspirant
inarticulate	ascribe	aspirate
artifice	ascribable	aspiration
artificer	ascription	aspirin
artificial	aseptic	assail
artficiality	ashamed	assailable
artillery	ashy	assailant
artisan	Asiatic	unassailable
artist	aside	unassailed
artistic	asinine	assassin
artistry	asininity	assassinate
inartistic	ask	assassination
Aryan	asked	assault
asbestos	unasked	assemble
ascend	askance	assemblage
ascendancy	asleep	assembly
ascendant	asparagus	assert
ascension	aspect	assertion
ascent	asperity	assertive
descend	asperse	assess
ascertain	aspersion	assessable
ascertainable	asphalt	assessed
ascertained	asphyxiate	assesses
ascertainment	asphyxiation	assessment

assessor	dissociate	astronomer
asseverate	assonance	astronomic
assiduous	assort	astute
assiduity	assorted	asylum
assign	assortment	atavism
assignable	assuage	atheism
assignat	assume	atheist
assigned	assumption	athlete
assignee	unassuming	athletic
assignment	assure	athletics
assignor	assurance	athwart
unassigned	assured	Atlantic
assimilate	assures	atmosphere
assimilable	reassure	atmospheric
assimilation	asterisk	atom
assimilative	asthma	atomic
unassimilated	astigmatism	atomize
assist	astonish	atone
assistance	astonished	atoned
assistant	astonishment	atonement
unassisted	astound	unatoned
assize	astrakhan	atrocious
associate	astringent	atrophy
association	astrology	attach
associative	astronomy	attached

attaches	attire	augury
attachment	attired	august
unattached	attitude	augustly
attain	attorney	August
attainable	attract	aureole
attained	attracted	aurora
attainment	attraction	auscultation
unattainable	attractive	auspices
attainder	unattractive	auspicious
attempt	attribute	inauspicious
attempted	auburn	austere
attend	auctioneer	austerity
attendance	audacious	authentic
attendant	audacity	authentically
attended	audible	authenticate
attention	audibility	authenticity
attentive	inaudible	unauthenticated
inattention	audience	author
inattentive	audit	authoritative
unattended	audition	authority
attenuate	auditor	authorization
attenuated	auditorium	authorize
attenuation	auditory	authorship
attest	augment	unauthorized
attestation	augmentative	autobiography

autochthonous	unavailable	avoidable
autocrat	avalanche	avoidance
autocracy	avarice	avoids
autocratic	avaricious	unavoidable
autograph	avenge	avoirdupois
autographed	avenue	avowal
automatic	aver	disavowal
automatism	average	aware
automaton	averse	unaware
automobile	aversion	awful
autonomy	avert	awkward
autopsy	aviation	awning
autosuggestion	aviator	axiom
autumn	avid	axiomatic
autumnal	avidity	axis
auxiliary	avidly	axle
available	avoid	azure

B

babbitt
babble
baccalaureate
bachelor
bacillus
bacilli
back
backbone
backer
background
backhand
backslider
backward
backwardness
backwash
bacterium
bacteria
bacterial
bacteriology
badinage
baffle
bag
bagasse
bagatelle

baggage
bagpipe
bail
bailiff
bailiwick
bailment
balance
unbalanced
balbriggan
balcony
baldachin
baldric
balk
ballast
unballasted
ballet
ballistics
balloon
ballot
balsam
baluster
balustrade
bamboo
banal
banality

banana
bandage
bandaged
bandanna
bandit
bandoleer
bang
banish
banishment
banister
bank
bankrupt
bankruptcy
banquet
banter
baptize
baptism
Baptist
bar
barred
barb
barbed
barbarian
barbaric
barbarism

barbarity	barrier	beatitude
barbarous	barrister	beauty
barbecue	base	beauteous
barber	basal	beauties
barbican	baseboard	beautiful
bargain	basement	beautify
bargained	bases	beaver
barge	basic	because, cause
baritone	basis	bed
barley	debase	bedchamber
barnacle	bashful	bedridden
barograph	bashfulness	bedroom
barometer	basilica	bedspread
barometric	basilisk	bee
baron	bassoon	befall
baroness	baton	befell
baronet	battalion	befit
baronial	battery	before
barrack	battle	beforehand
barrage	bayonet	befriend
barratry	bayou	beg
barrel	beacon	beggar
barren	beagle	begonia
barrenness	beatify	beguile
barricade	beatification	behalf

behave	belligerent	bereave
behaved	bellows	berth
behavior	belong	beseech
misbehave	belove	beside
behead	below	besiege
beheld	belt	bespeak
behest	bench	best
behind	beneath	bestial
behindhand	benediction	bestiality
behold	benefit	bestow
behoove	benefaction	bestowal
beige	benefactor	betray
belfry	beneficence	betrayal
belie	beneficent	betrayed
belief	beneficial	betroth
believable	beneficiary	betrothal
believes	benevolence	better
disbelieve	benevolent	bettered
unbelievable	malevolent	betterment
belittle	benign	between
bell	benignancy	bevel
bellicose	benignant	beveled
bellicosity	benzene	beverage
belligerence	bequeath	bewail
belligerency	bequest	beware

bewilder

bewilderment

bewitch

beyond

biannual

bibliography

bicameral

biceps

bicuspid

bicycle

bid

bidden

biennial

bigamy

bigot

bigotry

bijou

bilingual

bilious

bill, built

billboard

billhead

billiards

billow

bimetallism

binary

binnacle

binocular

biography

biology

biplane

birth

birthday

birthmark

rebirth

bisect

bishop

archbishop

bishopric

bismuth

bison

bite

bit

bitten

bitter

bitterest

bitumen

black

blackberry

blackboard

blacken

blackened

blackmail

blackness

blame

blamed

blameless

blameworthy

blandish

blandishment

blanket

blaspheme

blazon

blemish

unblemished

blight

blighted

blinder

blinker

bliss

blissful

blissfully

blissfulness

blister

blistered

blithesome	boast	bonus
blizzard	boastful	book
block	bodice	bookkeeper
blockade	bodkin	bookkeeping
blockhouse	body	booklet
blood	bodies	bookshelf
bloodless	bodily	boomerang
bloodshot	bodyguard	boracic
bloody	disembodied	border
blouse	embody	bordered
bludgeon	bog	borderless
bluff	bogus	borough
blunder	boiler	borrow
blundered	bold	bosom
blunderer	bolder	botany
blunt	boldest	botanic
blur	bolster	botanical
blush	bolt	botanist
unblushing	bolted	both
bluster	bombardment	bother
boa	bombastic	bothered
boar	bond	bothersome
board	bondage	bottle
boarded	bonded	bottled
boarder	bonnet	bottom

bough	braggart	brigand
boulevard	brandish	brigantine
bounce	brave	bright
bounced	bravery	brighten
bound	bravest	brighter
boundary	brazen	brightly
bounden	brazier	brightness
boundless	breadth	brilliant
unbounded	break	brilliance
bounty	breakable	brilliancy
bounteous	breakage	brilliantine
bounties	unbreakable	bristle
bountiful	unbroken	brocade
bouquet	breast	brochure
bovine	breath	brokerage
bower	brevet	bronchitis
bowlder	breviary	brother
bowsprit	brew	brother-in-law
box	bribery	brotherly
boxed	bride	brougham
boxer	bridal	brown
boxes	brief	brownish
boycott	abbreviate	brunt
bracelet	brevity	brush
brackish	brigade	brute

brutality	bulletin	burlesque
brutalization	bullion	burly
brutalize	bullock	burn
brutally	bulrush	burned
brutish	bulwark	burner
bubble	bunch	burnt
buccaneer	bundle	burnish
bucket	bungalow	burrow
buckle	bungle	bursar
buckler	bunion	burst
buckram	bunker	bury
bucolic	buoy	burial
budget	buoyancy	bush
buffalo	buoyant	business
buffet	burden	businesslike
bugle	burdened	bust
build	burdensome	bustle
builded	bureau	bustled
builder	bureaucracy	busy
built	bureaucrat	busied
bulb	bureaucratic	busily
bulge	burgess	but
bulk	burglar	butcher
bulky	burglarious	butler
bullet	burlap	butt

butter		buttonhook		by	
buttered		buttonwood		bygone	
butternut		buttress		by-law	
buttery		buxom		by-product	
button		buy		bystander	
buttoned		buyer		byway	
buttonhole		buzzard		byword	

C

cabal	miscalculate	canal
cabbage	calendar	canary
cabin	caliber	cancel
cabinet	calibrate	cancellation
cable	calico	cancer
cablegram	caliper	candelabrum
cadaver	calisthenics	candidate
cadence	call	candidacy
cadenza	recall	candidature
cadet	calliope	candle
caduceus	callous	candor
cafeteria	callosity	candid
caisson	calm	candy
cajole	calmed	candied
calamity	calmly	canine
calamitous	calmness	canister
calcium	calorie	canker
calcimine	calumny	canned
calcine	calumniate	cannery
calculate	calumnious	cannibal
calculable	cambric	cannon
calculation	camel	cannonade
calculator	campaign	cannoneer
incalculable	camphor	canny
	Canadian	canoe

canopy		recapitulate		carburetor	
cantaloupe		caprice		carcass	
canteen		capricious		carcinoma	
canter		capsize		cardboard	
cantilever		capstan		cardiac	
canton		capsule		cardinal	
canvas		captain		care	
caoutchouc		caption		careful	
capable		captious		careless	
capability		capture		carelessness	
capacious		captivate		cares	
capacitate		captivity		careworn	
capacity		captor		career	
incapable		carat		caress	
incapacitate		caravan		caribou	
incapacity		carbide		caricature	
capillary		carbine		carmine	
capillarity		carbolic		carnal	
capital		carbon		carnage	
capitalism		bicarbonate		carnival	
capitalist		carbohydrate		carnivorous	
capitalization		carbonic		incarnate	
capitalize		carbonization		incarnation	
capitally		carbonize		carol	
capitulate		carborundum		carom	

carouse		castigate		cathedral	
carp		castigated		catholic	
carpenter		castigation		catholicism	
carpet		casual		catholicity	
carriage		casually		non-catholic	
carrion		casualty		caucus	
carrot		casuist		cauliflower	
carry		cataclysm		cause, because	
carrier		catafalque		causal	
carries		catalepsy		causation	
cartage		catalogue		causative	
cartilage		catalysis		causes	
carton		catamount		caustic	
cartoon		catapult		cauterize	
cartouche		cataract		cauterization	
cartridge		catarrh		caution	
carve		catarrhal		cautionary	
caryatid		catastrophe		cautioned	
cascade		catastrophic		cautious	
cash		catechism		precaution	
cashable		catechize		cavalry	
cashed		category		cavalcade	
cashier		categorical		cavalier	
casino		catenary		cavern	
casserole		caterpillar		caviar	

cavil	celerity	center
cavity	accelerate	centigrade
cease	deceleration	centipede
ceased	celery	central
ceaseless	celestial	centralization
ceases	cellar	centralize
cessation	cello	decentralize
incessant	cellular	centrifugal
unceasing	celluloid	centripetal
cedar	cement	century
cede	cemetery	ceramic
accede	cenotaph	cerebellum
ceded	censer	cerebral
exceed	censor	cerement
intercede	censorious	ceremony
precede	censorship	ceremonial
proceed	uncensored	ceremonious
recede	censure	unceremonious
secede	censurable	certain
succeed	censured	ascertained
cedilla	censures	certainly
celebrate	census	certainty
celebrant	centenary	uncertain
celebration	centenarian	certify
celebrity	centennial	certificate

certification	chandelier	discharge
certiorari	change	chariot
certitude	changeable	charioteer
cessation	changeless	charity
incessant	exchange	charitable
cession	interchangeable	uncharitable
chagrin	unchanged	charlatan
chair	channel	charter
armchair	chant	chartered
chairman	chaos	chassis
chalcedony	chaotic	chasten
chalk	chapel	chastise
challenge	chaperon	chattel
challenger	chaplain	chauffeur
unchallenged	chapter	cheap
chamber	character	cheapen
chamberlain	characteristic	cheapened
chameleon	characterization	cheaper
chamois	characterize	cheapest
champagne	characterizes	cheapness
champion	charcoal	check
championship	charge	cheer
chancel	chargeable	cheered
chancellor	charged	cheerful
chancery	charger	cheerfulness

cheerless	chintz	Christendom
cheery	chipmunk	Christian
chemical	chisel	Christianity
chemist	chiseled	Christmas
chemistry	chivalry	chromatic
cherish	chivalric	achromatic
cherry	chivalrous	panchromatic
cherub	chlorine	chromium
chest	bichloride	chromate
chestnut	chlorate	chromic
chevron	chloride	chronic
chicken	chlorinate	chronicle
chide	chloroform	chronicler
chieftain	chocolate	chronograph
chiffon	choice	chronology
child	choices	chronometer
childhood	choir	chrysanthemum
childish	cholera	chunk
childlike	choose	church
children	chose	churl
grandchild	chosen	churn
chimera	chord	cicatrix
chimeric	chorus	cigar
chimerical	Christ	cigarette
chimney	christen	cincture

cinder	circumspection	uncivilized
incinerate	circumstance	claim
cinematograph	circumstances	acclaim
cinnamon	circumstantial	claimant
cinquefoil	circumstantially	claimed
cipher	circumvent	counterclaim
circle	circus	disclaim
circled	cistern	reclaim
circlet	citadel	unclaimed
encircle	cite	clairvoyance
circuit	citation	clamor
circuitous	incite	clamorous
circular	recite	clandestine
circularization	citizen	clangor
circularize	citizenry	clarify
circulate	citizens	clarification
circulated	citizenship	clarinet
circulation	citric	clarion
circulatory	citron	classic
circumference	civic	classical
circumflex	civil	classicist
circumlocution	civilian	classify
circumnavigate	civility	classification
circumscribe	civilization	unclassified
circumspect	civilize	clavicle

clavier

clean

  cleaned

  cleaner

  cleanest

  cleanliness

  cleanness

  unclean

clear

  clearage

  clearance

  cleared

  clearer

  clearest

  clearly

  clearness

  clears

cleave

  cleavage

  cleaver

clement

  clemency

  inclement

clergy

  clergyman

clerk

clerical

clever

  cleverer

  cleverest

client

  clientage

  clientele

climactic

climate

  acclimate

  climatic

climax

  anticlimax

clinic

  clinical

  clinician

clockwise

cloister

close

  closed

  closer

  closest

  disclose

  closet

closure

cloud

  cloudless

  clouds

  cloudy

  unclouded

clover

clown

club

clumsy

  clumsier

  clumsiest

  clumsily

  clumsiness

cluster

clutch

clutter

coach

coadjutor

coagulate

coal

coalesce

  coalescence

  coalescent

  coalition

coarse	coefficient	cohesive
coarsen	coerce	incoherent
coarseness	coercion	cohort
coarser	coercive	coiffure
coarsest	coeval	coinage
coast	coexecutor	coincide
coastal	coffee	coincidence
coastwise	coffer	coincident
co-author	coffin	coincidental
cobalt	cog	colander
cobble	cogent	coliseum
cobweb	cogency	collaborate
cocaine	cogitate	collaboration
cochineal	cogitation	collaborator
cockade	cogitative	collapse
cocktail	cognac	collapsible
cocoa	cognate	collar
coconut	cognizant	collate
cocoon	cognizance	collation
codefendant	cognomen	collateral
codfish	cohere	colleague
codicil	coherence	collect
codify	coherent	collectible
codification	coherer	collection
coeducation	cohesion	collective

collectorship	colossus	comic
uncollectible	colporteur	comical
college	column	comity
collegiate	columnar	comma
collide	coma	command
collision	comatose	commandant
collodion	combat	commandeer
colloid	combatant	commander
colloquy	combative	commandment
colloquial	non-combatant	commemorate
colloquialism	combine	commemoration
collusion	combination	commemorative
cologne	combined	commence
colonel	combines	commenced
colonnade	combustion	commencement
colony	combustibility	commend
colonial	come	commendable
colonist	comedy	commendation
colonization	comedian	commendatory
colonize	comet	commended
colophon	comfort	commensurate
color	comfortable	commensurable
colorless	comforter	comment
discolor	discomfort	commentary
colossal	uncomfortable	commentator

commented	communion	incomparable
commerce	communism	compartment
commercial	community	apartment
commercialism	communicate	department
commercialization	communicable	compass
commercialize	communicant	compassion
commiserate	communication	compassionate
commiseration	communicative	compatibility
commission	excommunicate	compatible
commissioned	uncommunicative	incompatible
commissioner	commute	compatriot
commissioners	commutation	compel
commit	commuter	compelled
commitment	compact	compulsion
committee	compactness	compulsory
commodious	companion	compendium
commodity	companionable	compendious
commodore	companionship	compensate
common	company	compensation
commoner	accompany	compensatory
commonly	compare	compete
commonwealth	comparable	competed
commotion	comparative	competes
commune	compared	competition
communal	comparison	competitive

competitor

competent

competence

competently

incompetent

compile

compilation

compiled

complacent

complacence

complacency

complain

complainant

complaint

complaisant

complement

complete

completion

incomplete

uncompleted

complex

complexity

complexion

complicate

complicated

complication

complicity

accomplice

compliment

complimentary

uncomplimentary

complin

comply

compliance

compliant

component

comport

compose

composedly

composer

composes

composite

composition

compositor

composure

compound

comprehend

comprehended

comprehensible

comprehension

comprehensive

incomprehensible

compress

compressible

compression

compressor

comprise

comprised

compromise

compromised

comptroller

compulsion

compulsory

compunction

compute

computation

computes

comrade

comradeship

concatenate

concatenation

concave

concavity

conceal

concealed

concealment

concede

conceded

concession

conceit

conceited

conceive

conceivable

concentrate

concentrated

concentration

concentric

concept

conception

concern

concerned

unconcerned

concert

concerted

disconcerted

preconcerted

concession

conch

conciliate

conciliation

conciliatory

irreconcilable

reconcile

reconciliation

concise

conciseness

conclave

conclude

conclusion

conclusive

inconclusive

concoct

concocted

concoction

concomitant

concord

concordance

discord

concourse

concrete

concur

concurrence

concurrent

condemn

condemnation

condemnatory

condemned

condense

condensation

condensed

condenser

condenses

condescend

condescended

condescension

condign

condiment

condition

conditional

conditionally

recondition

unconditional

condolence

condone

condonation

conduce

conducive

conduct

conducted

conductivity

conductor	confidentially	confounded
misconduct	confidently	confront
conduit	confine	confronted
cone	confined	confuse
conic	confinement	confused
conical	unconfined	confuses
confection	confirm	confusion
confectioner	affirm	confute
confectionery	confirmation	confutation
confederate	confirmed	congeal
confederacy	unconfirmed	congealed
confederation	confiscate	congenial
confer	confiscated	congeniality
conferee	confiscation	uncongeniality
conference	confiscatory	congest
conferred	conflagration	congested
confess	conflict	congestion
confession	confliction	congests
confessional	confluence	conglomerate
confessor	conform	conglomeration
confide	conformable	congratulate
confidant	conformation	congratulated
confidence	conformed	congratulation
confident	conformity	congratulatory
confidential	confound	congregate

congregated	disconnected	consent
congregation	unconnected	consented
congregational	connivance	consequence
gregarious	connoisseur	consequent
segregate	connotation	consequential
congress	conquer	inconsequential
congressional	conqueror	conserve
congruous	unconquerable	conservation
incongruous	unconquered	conservatism
conjecture	conquest	conservative
conjectural	conquests	conservatory
conjugal	consanguinity	conserved
conjugate	conscience	consider
conjugated	conscientious	considerable
conjugation	conscious	considerate
conjunction	consciousness	consideration
conjuncture	unconscious	considers
conjure	conscript	inconsiderate
conjured	conscription	unconsidered
conjurer	consecrate	consign
conjures	consecrated	consigned
connect	consecration	consignee
connected	unconsecrated	consignment
connection	consecutive	consignor
connective	consensus	consist

consistence	constant	consult
consistency	constancy	consultant
consistent	constellation	consultation
consists	consternation	consults
inconsistent	constitute	consume
console	constituency	consumed
consolation	constituent	consumer
consoles	constitution	consummate
disconsolate	constitutional	consummation
inconsolable	constitutionality	consumption
consolidate	constitutionally	consumptive
consolidated	unconstitutional	contact
consolidation	constrain	contagion
consonant	constraint	contagious
consonance	unconstrained	contain
consort	constrict	contained
consorted	constrictor	container
conspicuous	construct	contaminate
conspicuously	constructed	contamination
inconspicuous	constructive	uncontaminated
conspire	misconstruction	contemplate
conspiracy	construe	contemplated
conspirator	construed	contemplation
constable	consul	contemplative
constabulary	consulate	contemporaneous

contemporary	continual	contrast
contempt	continually	contrasted
contemptible	continuance	contravene
contemptuous	continuation	contravention
contend	continued	contribute
contended	continuity	contribution
contention	continuous	contributor
content	discontinue	contributory
contented	contort	contrite
contentment	contorted	contrition
discontented	contortion	contrived
contest	contour	contrivance
contestant	contraband	control
contestation	contract	controlled
contested	contracted	controller
contests	contraction	uncontrollable
incontestable	contractor	controvert
context	contradict	controversial
contiguous	contradiction	controversy
contiguity	contradictory	incontroverted
continent	uncontradicted	incontrovertible
continental	contradistinction	contumacy
contingent	contraption	contumacious
contingency	contrary	contumely
continue	contrariness	contused

contusion	converses	convulsive
conundrum	convert	cookery
convalescence	conversion	cooperate
convalescent	converted	cooperation
convection	convertible	cooperative
convene	convex	coordinate
convention	convexity	coordination
reconvene	convey	copartnership
convenience	conveyance	copious
conveniences	conveyed	copper
convenient	conveyer	copy
inconvenienced	convict	copyist
inconvenient	conviction	copyright
convent	convince	cordage
conventual	convinced	cordial
convention	convivial	cordiality
conventional	conviviality	corduroy
unconventional	convoke	cork
converge	convocation	corn
convergent	convoked	cornstarch
converse	convolution	corner
conversant	convoy	cornet
conversation	convoyed	cornice
conversational	convulse	corona
conversed	convulsion	coroner

coronet	correspond	cosmetic
coronation	correspondence	cosmic
corporal	correspondent	cosmopolitan
corporate	corresponds	cost
corporately	corridor	costliness
corporation	corroborate	costly
incorporate	corroboration	costume
corporeal	corroborative	costumed
corps	uncorroborated	costumer
corpse	corrode	cosy
corpulence	corrosion	cosily
corpuscle	corrosive	cosiness
correct	corrugate	cotemporaneous
corrected	corrugation	contemporaneous
correction	corrupt	coterie
corrective	corruption	cottage
correctly	corruptly	cotton
correctness	incorruptible	couch
corrector	corset	cougar
incorrect	cortex	could
uncorrected	corundum	council
correlate	carborundum	councilor
correlated	coruscate	count
correlation	coruscation	counted
correlative	coryza	countess

countless	courageous	recover
uncounted	discourage	uncover
countenance	encouragement	covert
discountenance	courier	covetous
counter	course	coward
counteract	concourse	cowardice
counterbalance	courser	cowboy
counterclaim	courses	cowl
counterfeit	discourse	coxswain
counterfeited	discursive	cracker
counterirritant	recourse	cranberry
countermand	court	cranium
countermanded	courted	cranial
countermine	courthouse	craziness
countermined	courtliness	create
counterpart	court-martial	created
counterpoint	courtyard	creation
country	courteous	creative
countryside	courtesy	creator
county	cousin	creature
coupé	covenant	recreation
couple	cover	credence
coupled	coverlet	credential
coupon	discover	credible
courage	discovery	credibility

credulity	cripple	coronet
credulous	crisis	crowned
incredible	crises	crucial
incredulity	criterion	crucible
incredulous	criteria	crucifix
credit	critic	crucifixion
creditable	criticism	crucify
creditor	criticize	crude
credits	criticizes	crudely
discreditable	critics	crudity
cremate	crochet	cruel
cremation	crocodile	cruelly
crematory	crocus	cruelty
creole	crop	cruise
creosote	croquet	cruised
crescendo	crosier	cruiser
crescent	cross	cruises
crestfallen	crossed	crumb
cretonne	crosses	crumble
crevice	crossroad	crumple
crew	crouch	crusade
cribbage	crowd	crusader
criminal	crowded	crutch
crimson	crowds	crux
crinoline	crown	crypt

cryptic	cultivated	curb
cryptogram	cultivates	curd
crystal	cultivation	cure
crystalline	cultivator	curable
crystallization	uncultivated	curative
crystallize	culture	cures
cube	cultural	incurable
cubed	cultured	curfew
cubic	uncultured	curious
cubical	culvert	curiosity
cuckoo	cumbrous	curiously
cucumber	cumbersome	curl
cudgel	encumber	curly
cuisine	encumbrance	currant
culinary	unencumbered	currency
culminate	cumulative	current
culminated	accumulate	curriculum
culmination	cuneiform	curricula
culpable	cunning	curse
culpability	cupboard	cursive
culprit	cupful	cursory
exculpate	cupidity	curtail
inculpate	cupola	curtain
cult	curate	curve
cultivate	curator	curvature

curved		customs		cylindrical	
cushion		cutaneous		cymbal	
cushioned		cuticle		cynic	
cuspidor		subcutaneous		cynically	
custard		cutlery		cynicism	
custody		cutlet		cynosure	
custodian		cycle		cyst	
custom		cyclone		cystoid	
accustomed		cyclopedia		czar	
customary		cyclopedic		czarina	
customer		encyclopedia		czarism	
customhouse		cylinder		Czech	

D

dachshund
daffodil
daguerreotype
dainty
daintier
daintiest
daintily
dalliance
damage
damaged
indemnify
undamaged
damask
damp
dampen
dampener
damper
dampness
dance
danced
dancer
dandelion
dandy
danger

dangerous
dangers
endangered
dare
dared
dares
dark
darken
darkness
data
datum
date
dated
undated
dative
daughter
daughter-in-law
granddaughter
daunt
dauntless
undaunted
davenport
davit
day
daydream

daylight
days
daytime
dazzle
dazzled
dead
deaden
deadened
deadeye
deadfall
deadliness
deaf
deafened
deafness
deal
dealer
deals
dealt
dear
dearer
dearest
dearly
dears
deary
endeared

dearth	decanter	decisiveness
death	decapitate	indecision
deathbed	decapitation	undecided
deathless	decathlon	decimal
deathlike	decease	decimate
deathly	deceased	decipher
debacle	decedent	decipherable
debate	deceit	undecipherable
debatable	deceitful	declaim
debated	deceive	declamation
debater	deceiver	declamatory
debenture	deceives	declare
debilitate	deception	declarable
debilitated	deceptive	declaration
debilitation	decent	declarative
debility	decency	declaratory
debonair	decently	decline
debt	indecency	declension
debit	indecent	declined
debtor	decide	declivity
indebtedness	decidedly	incline
début	decides	recline
decade	decision	decoction
decadence	decisive	decompose
decalcomania	decisively	decomposed

decomposition	deed	defendant
decorate	deeded	defended
decoration	misdeed	defender
decorative	deep	defense
decorator	deepen	defenseless
decorum	deepness	defensible
decorous	depth	defensive
decoy	deer	defer
decoyed	deface	deference
decrease	efface	deferential
decreased	defalcate	deficiency
decree	defalcation	deficient
decrepit	defalcator	deficit
decrepitude	defame	defile
dedicate	defamation	define
dedication	defamatory	definable
dedicator	default	definite
dedicatory	defaulted	definiteness
deduce	defaulter	definition
deduces	defeat	definitive
deducible	defeated	indefinable
deduct	defect	indefinitely
deductible	defection	deflate
deduction	defective	deflation
deductively	defend	deform

deformed

deformity

defraud

defrauded

defray

defrayal

deft

defunct

defy

defiance

defiant

defied

degenerate

degeneracy

degeneration

degrade

degradation

degraded

degree

dehydrate

deify

deification

deifies

deism

deist

deity

deject

dejectedly

dejection

delay

delectable

delectation

delegate

delegation

delete

deletion

deleterious

deliberate

deliberately

deliberation

deliberative

delicate

delicacy

delicatessen

indelicate

delicious

delight

delighted

delightful

delineate

delineation

delineator

delinquent

delinquency

delirium

delirious

deliver

deliverable

deliverance

deliverer

delivery

undeliverable

delude

deluded

delusion

delusive

deluge

demagogue

demand

demarcation

demeanor

demented

dementia

demerit

demise

demobilize	denizen	compartment
demobilization	denominate	department
demobilized	denominated	departmental
democrat	denomination	departure
democracy	denominator	depend
democratic	denote	dependable
democratically	denounce	depended
demolish	denouncement	dependence
demolition	denouncer	dependent
demon	denunciation	independence
demonetize	denunciatory	independent
demonetization	dense	depict
demonstrate	density	depicted
demonstrable	dental	deplete
demonstrative	dentist	depleted
demonstrator	dentistry	depletion
demoralize	deny	deplore
demoralization	denial	deplorability
demoralized	denied	deplorable
demur	denier	deponent
demurrer	denies	depopulate
demurrage	undeniable	deport
demure	deodorize	deportation
denature	depart	deported
denim	apartment	deportment

depose	depute	descriptive
deposes	deputation	desecrate
deposit	deputize	desecration
depositary	deputy	desert
deposition	derange	deserted
depositor	derangement	deserter
depository	derelict	desertion
depot	dereliction	deserve
deprave	deride	deservedly
depravation	derision	undeserved
depravity	derisive	desiccate
deprecate	derive	desiccation
deprecation	derivation	desiccator
deprecatory	derivative	design
depreciate	derogation	designate
depreciation	derogative	designation
depredation	derogatory	designed
depress	derrick	designer
depressant	descend	desire
depression	ascend	desirable
depressive	descendant	desires
deprive	descent	desirous
deprivation	describe	undesirable
privation	describable	desist
depth	description	desisted

desists	destroy	determine
desolate	destroyed	determination
desolately	destroyer	determinedly
desolation	destruction	indeterminate
despair	destructive	predetermined
despaired	desuetude	undetermined
desperate	desultory	detest
desperately	desultorily	detestable
desperation	detach	detestation
despise	detached	dethrone
despicable	detachment	dethroned
despite	detail	detonate
despond	detailed	detonation
despondency	detain	detour
despondent	detained	detract
despot	detention	detraction
despotic	detect	detractor
despotism	detected	detriment
dessert	detective	detrimental
destine	detector	devastate
destination	deter	devastation
destined	deterrent	develop
destiny	deteriorate	developer
destitute	deteriorated	development
destitution	deterioration	undeveloped

deviate	diagnostic	dictograph
deviated	diagnostician	dictum
deviation	diagonal	dicta
devious	diagonally	dictums
device	diagram	didactic
devised	diagrammatic	diet
devil	dialect	dietary
devoid	dialectics	dietetics
devolve	dialogue	differ
devote	diameter	difference
devotee	diametric	different
devotion	diametrically	differential
devotional	diamond	differentially
devout	diapason	differentiate
dexterous	diaphanous	differentiation
ambidextrous	diaphragm	differently
dexterity	diatribe	indifferent
diabetes	dictaphone	difficult
diabetic	dictate	difficulties
diabolical	dictation	difficulty
diacritical	dictator	diffident
diadem	dictatorial	diffidence
diaeresis	dictatorially	diffraction
diagnose	diction	diffuse
diagnosis	dictionary	diffuses

diffusible	dilemma	dingy
diffusion	diligent	dinosaur
digest	diligence	dint
digestible	dilute	diocese
digestion	diluted	diphtheria
digestive	dilution	diphtheritic
indigestion	undiluted	diphthong
undigested	dim	diphthongal
digit	dimly	diploma
digital	dimmed	diplomat
digitalis	dimmer	diplomacy
dignify	dimness	diplomatic
dignitary	undimmed	diplomatist
dignity	dimension	dipsomania
indignity	dimensional	dipsomaniac
undignified	diminish	dire
digress	diminuendo	direful
digression	diminution	direly
digressive	diminutive	direct
dike	undiminished	direction
dilapidate	dimity	directness
dilapidation	dimple	director
dilate	dine	directorate
dilation	dined	directory
dilatory	dinner	indirect

undirected

dirigible

disable

disability

disabuse

disadvantage

disadvantageous

disaffected

disaffection

disagree

disagreeable

disagreed

disagreement

disallow

disappear

disappearance

disappoint

disappointment

disapprobation

disapprove

disapproval

disarm

disarrange

disarticulate

disaster

disastrous

disavow

disavowal

disband

disbelieve

disbeliever

disbursement

discard

discarded

discern

discernible

discernment

discharge

discharged

disciple

disciplinary

discipline

disclaim

disclaimed

disclaimer

disclose

disclosed

discloses

disclosure

undisclosed

discolor

discoloration

discomfiture

discomfort

discompose

discomposes

discomposure

disconcert

disconcertedly

discontent

discontented

discontinue

discontinuance

discontinued

discord

concord

discordant

discount

discountenance

discourage

discouraged

discouragement

encourage

discourse

discursive

discourteous	disentangle	disinherit
discover	disfavor	disintegrate
discoverer	disfeature	disinterested
discovery	disfigure	disjoin
discreditable	disfranchise	disjunction
discreet	disgrace	disjunctive
discretion	disgraceful	dislike
indiscreet	disguise	dislocate
discrepancy	undisguised	dislodge
discriminate	disgust	disloyal
discriminated	dishabille	dismal
discrimination	dishearten	dismantle
discriminatory	dishevel	dismay
indiscriminate	dishonor	undismayed
discuss	dishonest	dismember
discussion	dishonestly	dismiss
disdain	dishonesty	dismissal
disdained	dishonorable	dismissed
disdainful	disillusion	dismount
diseased	disincline	disobey
disembark	disinclination	disobedience
disembarcation	disinclined	disobedient
disenchant	disinfect	disobeyed
disengage	disinfectant	disoblige
disengagement	disingenuous	disorderly

disorganize	dispossess	dissemination
disparage	disproportion	dissent
disparagement	disproportionate	dissension
disparate	disprove	dissented
disparity	disproof	dissenter
dispassionate	dispute	dissertation
dispatch	disputation	dissidence
dispatched	disputatious	dissimilar
dispatcher	disputes	dissimilarity
dispel	undisputed	dissimulate
dispelled	disqualify	dissipate
dispense	disqualification	dissociate
dispensable	disquisition	dissolute
dispensary	disregard	dissoluble
dispensation	disrepute	dissolution
dispensed	disreputable	indissoluble
disperse	disrespect	dissonant
dispersal	disrupt	dissonance
dispersion	disruption	dissuade
displacement	dissatisfy	dissuasion
disport	dissatisfaction	persuade
dispose	dissect	suasion
disposal	dissection	distant
disposes	dissemble	distance
disposition	disseminate	distaste

distasteful	distributive	diversification
distend	distributor	diversify
distensible	redistribute	diversion
distension	undistributed	diversity
distill	district	divert
distillate	redistricted	divest
distillation	distrust	divide
distillery	distrusted	divided
distinct	distrustful	dividend
distinction	disturb	divider
distinctive	disturbance	divisible
distinguish	disturbed	division
distinguishable	disturber	divisor
indistinct	undisturbed	indivisible
indistinguishable	disuse	undivided
distort	ditto	divine
distorted	diurnal	divination
distortion	divagate	divined
distract	divagation	divinity
distrain	divan	divorce
distraught	diverge	divorcée
distress	divergence	divulge
distressed	divergent	dizzy
distribute	divers	dizzily
distribution	diverse	dizziness

docile	dominant	dower
docility	domination	dowager
docket	domineer	down
dockyard	dominion	downcast
doctor	predominate	downfall
doctorate	domino	downright
doctrine	donate	downward
doctrinaire	donated	doxology
doctrinal	donation	dozen
document	donor	draft
documentary	donkey	dragon
doge	door	dragoon
dogma	doorway	drainage
dogmatic	dooryard	drama
dogmatize	dormant	dramatic
doldrums	dormer	dramatist
dollar	dormitory	dramatization
domain	dormouse	dramatize
domestic	double	drapery
domesticate	doubt	drastic
domesticated	doubted	draw
domesticity	doubtful	drawback
domicile	doubtless	drawbridge
dominate	doubts	drawee
dominance	undoubted	drawer

drawn	drunken	duplicator
dread	drunkenness	duplicity
dreaded	dry	durable
dreadful	drier	durability
dreadnaught	driest	during
dream	dryly	duration
dreamed	dryness	dust
dreamer	dry-shod	duty
dreamily	dual	duteous
drift	dubiety	dutiable
driveway	dubious	duties
dromedary	indubitable	dutiful
droop	duchess	undutiful
drop	ductile	dwarf
drought	ductility	dwell
drown	duel	dwelt
drowned	duly	dwindle
drudge	unduly	dwindled
drudgery	dumb	dynamic
drug	dump	dynamite
druggist	dungeon	dynamo
drum	duplex	dynasty
drunk	duplicate	dyspepsia
drunkard	duplication	dyspeptic

E

each	easier	eclipsed
eager	easiest	economy
eagerly	easily	economic
eagerness	easiness	economical
ear	uneasiness	economist
eardrum	uneasy	economize
earmark	east	ecstasy
earldom	eastern	ecstatic
early	easterner	eczema
earlier	eastward	edible
earliest	eat	edibility
earnest	eatable	inedible
earnestly	eaten	edifice
earnestness	eater	edification
earth	uneaten	edify
earthen	ebony	edit
earthenware	ebullient	edition
earthliness	ebullience	editor
earthquake	ebullition	editorial
earthward	eccentric	editorially
earthwork	eccentricity	unedited
earthworm	ecclesiastic	educate
unearth	éclat	education
ease	eclectic	educational
	eclipse	educator

uneducated	effort	elaboration
efface	effortless	elastic
deface	effrontery	elasticity
effacement	effulgent	elect
effect	effusion	election
effective	effusive	electioneer
effectual	ego	elective
effectually	egoism	elector
effectuate	egoist	electoral
effectuation	egotism	electorate
ineffectual	egotist	reelect
effeminate	egotistic	electric
effeminacy	egregious	electrical
effervesce	egress	electrician
effervescence	congress	electricity
effervescent	ingress	electrification
efficacious	progress	electrify
efficacy	transgress	electrocute
efficient	either	electrode
efficiency	ejaculate	electrolier
inefficiency	eject	electrolysis
inefficient	ejection	electrolyte
efflorescent	inject	electromagnet
efflux	reject	electron
influx	elaborate	electroplate

electrotype		eliminated		emaciate	
eleemosynary		elimination		emaciated	
elegant		eliminative		emaciation	
elegance		elite		emanate	
elegantly		elixir		emanated	
inelegant		ellipse		emanation	
element		ellipsis		emancipate	
elemental		ellipsoid		emancipation	
elementally		elliptic		emancipator	
elementary		elliptical		embankment	
elephant		elocution		embargo	
elephantine		elocutionist		embarkation	
elevate		elongate		embarrass	
elevated		elongation		embarrassed	
elevation		eloquent		embarrasses	
elevator		eloquence		embarrassment	
elicit		grandiloquent		embassy	
elicitation		else		ambassador	
elicited		elsewhere		embezzle	
elide		elucidate		embezzled	
elision		elucidation		embezzlement	
eligible		elude		embezzler	
eligibility		elusion		emblem	
ineligible		elusive		emblematic	
eliminate		elusory		embody	

embodies	emissary	empty
embodiment	emit	emptied
embolden	emission	emptiest
emboldened	emollient	emptiness
embrace	emolument	emulate
embroider	emotion	emulous
embroideries	emotional	emulsify
embroidery	emotionally	emulsion
embryonic	unemotional	enable
emendation	emperor	inability
emerald	empress	unable
emerge	emphasis	enact
emerged	emphasized	enactment
emergence	emphasizes	reenact
emergency	emphatic	enamel
emergent	empire	enameled
emeritus	empiric	encampment
emigrate	empirical	enchant
emigrant	empiricism	enchanted
emigration	employ	enchantment
immigrate	employee	encircle
eminent	employer	enclose
eminence	employment	enclosure
eminently	unemployment	encomium
imminent	emporium	encomiastic

encore	unendorsed	engage
encounter	endow	disengage
encountered	endowed	engagement
encounters	endowment	engages
encourage	unendowed	reengage
discourage	endure	engine
encouraged	endurable	engineer
encouragement	endurance	English
encourages	unendurable	engraver
encroachment	enemy	engross
encumbrance	enmity	enhance
encyclical	inimical	enhancement
encyclopedia	energy	unenhanced
encyclopedic	energetic	enigma
end	energize	enigmatic
ended	enfeeble	enjoin
endless	enfold	enjoined
unending	enforce	injunction
endanger	enforceable	enjoy
endangered	enforced	enjoyable
endearment	enforcement	enjoyed
endeavor	enforces	enjoyment
endemic	reenforce	enjoys
endorse	enfranchise	enlarge
endorsement	enfranchisement	enlarged

enlargement	enslave	enthroned
enlighten	ensue	enthusiasm
enlightened	ensued	enthusiast
enlightenment	ensues	enthusiastic
unenlightened	entablature	enthusiastically
enlist	entail	unenthusiastic
enlistment	entailed	entice
enlists	entangle	enticed
reenlists	disentangled	entices
enliven	enter	entire
enmity	entered	entirely
ennoble	enters	entirety
ennoblement	entrance	entitle
ennui	entrant	entity
enormous	entry	entomb
enormity	reenter	entombed
enormously	enterprise	entombment
enough	unenterprising	entomology
enrapture	entertain	entrain
enrich	entertained	entrance
enriched	entertainer	entrap
enrichment	entertainment	entreat
ensconce	enthrall	entrust
ensign	enthralled	entry
ensilage	enthrone	entryway

entwine

entwined

enumerate

enumeration

enumerator

enunciate

enunciation

enunciator

envelope

envelopment

environs

environment

envoy

envy

enviable

envious

unenviable

enzyme

epaulette

ephemeral

ephemerally

epic

epical

epicure

epicurean

epidemic

epidermic

epidermis

epiglottis

epigram

epilepsy

epileptic

epilogue

episcopal

episcopalian

episode

episodic

epistle

epitaph

epithelium

epithet

epitome

epitomize

epoch

epochal

equable

equability

equal

equality

equalization

equalize

equally

unequaled

equanimity

equation

equator

equatorial

equestrian

equiangular

equidistant

equilateral

equilibrium

equilibrist

equine

equinox

equinoctial

equip

equipage

equipment

equity

equitable

inequitable

inequity

equivalent

equivocal

equivocate	erratic	escrow
equivocation	erratum	escutcheon
equivocator	inerrant	especial
eradicate	unerringly	especially
eradicable	errand	espionage
eradication	error	esplanade
ineradicable	erroneous	espouse
erase	erudite	espousal
erasable	erudition	esprit
eraser	erupt	esquire
erasure	eruption	essayist
erect	eruptive	essence
erectile	erysipelas	essential
erectility	escalator	essentially
erection	escapade	quintessence
erectness	escape	establishment
erector	escaped	estate
ergo	escapement	esteem
ermine	inescapable	esteemed
erode	escheat	estimable
erosion	eschew	inestimable
erosive	eschewal	esthetic
err	escort	estimate
aberration	escorted	estimated
errata	unescorted	estimation

estimator	euphemistic	uneventful
estop	euphony	ever
estoppel	evacuate	whatever
estranged	evacuated	whenever
estrangement	evacuation	wherever
estuary	evade	whichever
etch	evaded	every
eternal	evasion	everybody
eternally	evasive	everything
eternity	evaluate	everywhere
ether	evaluated	evict
ethereal	evaluation	eviction
etherealize	evanescent	evident
ethics	evanescence	evidence
ethical	evangelist	evil
unethical	evangelical	evilly
ethnic	evaporate	evince
ethnology	evaporation	evoke
ethyl	evening	evocation
etymology	event	evolve
eucalyptus	eventful	evolution
euchre	eventual	evolutionist
eulogy	eventuality	exacerbation
eulogize	eventually	exact
euphemism	eventuate	exaction

exactitude		excellency		exclude	
exactness		excellent		excluded	
inexact		excelsior		exclusion	
exaggeration		except		exclusive	
exalt		exceptionable		include	
exaltation		unexceptionable		included	
exalted		excerpt		excommunicate	
examine		excess		excoriate	
examination		excessive		excrescence	
example		exchange		excruciate	
exemplary		exchangeable		exculpate	
exemplification		exchequer		exculpation	
exemplify		excise		exculpatory	
sample		excision		excursion	
unexampled		excite		excuse	
exasperate		excitability		excusable	
exasperation		excitable		excuses	
excavate		excitant		inexcusable	
excavation		excitation		execrate	
excavator		excitement		execrable	
exceed		exciter		execration	
exceeded		exclaim		execute	
excel		exclaimed		executant	
excelled		exclamation		execution	
excellence		exclamatory		executioner	

executive	exhibition	exorbitant
executor	exhibitor	exordium
executrix	exhilarate	exoteric
exemplify	exhilaration	esoterical
exemplar	exhort	exotic
exemplary	exhortation	expand
exemplification	exhorted	expanse
exempt	exhume	expansible
exemption	exhumation	expansion
exequatur	exhumed	expansive
exercise	inhume	expatiate
exercises	exigent	expatiated
exert	exigency	expatiation
exerted	exiguous	expatriate
exertion	exile	expect
exhale	exiled	expectancy
exhalation	exist	expectant
exhaust	existence	expectation
exhaustible	existent	unexpectedly
exhaustion	exit	expectorate
exhaustive	exodus	expedient
exhaustless	ex officio	expedience
inexhaustible	exonerate	expedite
exhibit	exoneration	expedition
exhibited	exonerative	expeditious

expel

expelled

expulsion

expend

expenditure

expense

expensive

experience

inexperienced

experiment

experimental

experimentation

experimenter

expert

expiate

expiation

expiatory

expire

expiration

explain

explainable

explanation

explanatory

expletive

explicable

inexplicable

explicit

explode

explosion

exploit

exploitation

explore

exploration

exploratory

exponent

exponential

export

exportable

exportation

exported

exporter

expose

exposes

exposition

expositor

expository

expostulate

expound

express

expressage

expressible

expression

expressive

expressman

unexpressed

expropriate

expropriation

expulsion

expulsive

expunge

expurgate

exquisite

extant

extempore

extemporaneous

extemporary

extemporization

extemporize

extend

extended

extension

extensive

extent

extenuate

extenuated

extenuation	extract	extrude
exterior	extractable	exuberant
exterminate	extraction	exuberancy
extermination	extractive	exult
exterminator	extractor	exultant
external	extradite	exultation
externally	extraditible	exulted
extinct	extradition	eye
extinction	extraneous	eyeball
extinguish	extraordinary	eyebar
extinguishable	extraordinarily	eyebrow
extirpate	extravagant	eyeglass
extirpation	extravagance	eyelash
extol	extravaganza	eyelet
extolled	extreme	eyelid
extort	extremist	eyepiece
extorted	extremity	eyes
extortion	extricate	eyesight
extortionate	extrication	eyesore
extra	extrinsic	eyetooth

F

fable
fabulous
fabric
fabricate
fabrication
facade
face
facet
facial
facetious
facile
facilely
facilitate
facility
facsimile
fact
faction
factional
factious
factitious
factor
factory
facultative
faculty

manufacture
Fahrenheit
fail
failed
failure
faith
faithfulness
faithless
unfaithful
falcon
fall
fallen
fallacy
fallacious
fallible
infallible
false
falsehood
falsification
falsify
falsity
falter
fame
defame
famous

infamy
familiar
familiarity
familiarization
familiarize
familiarly
unfamiliar
family
families
famine
famish
fanatic
fanaticism
fanatics
fancy
fancier
fanciest
fanciful
fantasy
fantasia
fantastic
far
farsighted
farther
farthest

farm
farmed
farmers
farmhouse
farmyard
farthing
fascinate
fascinated
fascination
fashion
fashionable
old-fashioned
unfashionable
fast
fasten
faster
fastest
fastidious
fatal
fatality
fatally
father
fatherhood
father-in-law
fatherland

fatherless
fathom
fatigue
fatuous
fatuity
faucet
fault
faultily
faultless
faulty
favor
disfavor
favorable
favorite
favoritism
favors
unfavorable
fealty
fear
fearful
fearless
fearsome
feasible
feasibility
feast

feather
featherweight
feature
disfeature
febrile
federal
confederate
federacy
federalist
federalize
federate
federation
feeble
enfeeble
feebleness
felicitate
felicitous
felicity
feline
felon
felonious
felony
female
feminine
femininity

femur	festoon	filter
fender	fetish	filtered
ferment	fever	filtration
fermentable	feverish	filth
fermentation	fiasco	final
unfermented	fiat	finalist
ferocious	fiber	finality
ferocity	fibrous	finally
ferric	fickle	finance
ferrous	fiction	financial
ferrule	fictional	financier
fertile	fictitious	find
fertility	fidelity	finder
fertilization	infidel	finds
fertilize	perfidy	fine
fertilizer	fiduciary	fined
fervor	field	fineness
effervesce	fiend	finery
fervency	fiendish	refinery
fervent	figure	finger
fervid	disfigure	fingerling
festal	figurative	finis
festival	figurehead	finish
festive	transfigure	unfinished
festivity	filament	finite

infinite		fit		flannel	
infinitesimal		fitful		flash	
infinitive		fitly		flashily	
infinity		fitness		flashy	
fire		fix		flask	
fiery		affix		flatiron	
firearm		fixation		flatter	
firebrand		fixative		flattered	
firefly		fixes		flatterer	
fireman		fixity		flatters	
fire plug		fixture		flattery	
fireproof		prefix		flaunt	
fireside		suffix		flavor	
firm		transfix		flavorous	
firmness		flaccid		flaxen	
firmament		flagellate		fleet	
first		flagrant		flex	
fiscal		flagrance		flexibility	
fish		flagrancy		flexible	
fisherman		flame		flexor	
fishery		flamboyant		flexure	
fishhook		inflammation		inflexible	
fishy		flamingo		flicker	
fissure		flange		flight	
fist		flank		flighty	

flinch	flush	follows
fling	flute	fomentation
flint	flutter	fond
flippant	fluttered	fondest
flirtation	fluttery	fondness
float	fly	fondant
flotation	flight	fondle
flotsam	flyer	fool
flounce	flywheel	foolhardy
flounder	focus	foolish
flour	foci	foolscap
flourish	focuses	foot
flower	fodder	football
florist	foghorn	footboard
fluctuate	foible	footbridge
fluctuated	foil	footgear
fluctuation	foist	foothill
fluent	fold	foothold
fluency	folio	footlights
fluid	foliage	footnote
fluidity	foliation	footpath
fluidrachm	portfolio	footprint
flume	folk	footsore
fluorine	follow	footstep
fluorescent	follower	footstool

for	forefinger	forgetful
forage	foregone	forgettable
forasmuch	foreground	forgot
foray	foreign	unforgettable
forbear	foreigner	forgive
forbearance	foreknowledge	forgave
forbore	foremost	forgivable
forbid	forename	forgiven
forbidden	forenoon	unforgivable
force	foreordain	unforgiven
enforce	forerunner	forgo
forced	forest	fork
forceful	forestry	forlorn
forces	foretell	form
reenforce	foretold	conform
forceps	forethought	deform
forcible	forewoman	formal
forearm	forfeit	formality
forebear	forfeiture	formally
foreboding	forgather	format
forecast	forge	formation
forecaster	forged	formative
forecastle	forger	formerly
foreclose	forgery	informal
foreclosure	forget	uniform

formaldehyde	foul	fraternity
formidable	foulard	fraternal
formula	found	fraternally
formulate	foundation	fraternize
forsake	founded	fraud
forsooth	founder	defrauded
forswear	foundry	fraudulent
forthcoming	fount	free
forthright	fountain	freed
forthwith	foursome	freedom
fortify	fowl	freely
fortification	fox	freeness
fortress	fracas	freight
unfortified	fractional	freighter
fortitude	fracture	frequent
fortnight	fragile	frequency
fortuitous	fragility	frequently
fortune	fragment	fresh
fortunate	fragmentary	freshen
misfortune	frailty	freshly
unfortunate	franchise	freshman
forward	disfranchise	freshness
forwarder	enfranchise	fretwork
fossil	frantic	friable
foster	frenetic	friend

friendless	frosted	fully
friendly	frosty	fulminate
friendship	froth	fulmination
unfriendly	froward	fulsome
frigate	frown	fume
fright	frowned	fumigate
frighten	frugal	fumigation
frightened	fruit	perfume
frightful	fruitful	function
frigid	fruition	functional
frigidity	fruitless	fundamental
frigidly	frustrate	funereal
refrigerator	frustration	fungus
fringe	fuchsia	fungi
frivolity	fudge	funnel
frivolous	fuel	fur
frock	fugitive	furlough
frolic	fugacious	furnace
front	refuge	furnish
frontage	fulcrum	furnisher
frontal	fulfill	furnishings
fronted	fulfillment	furniture
frontier	unfulfilled	unfurnished
frontispiece	full	furor
frost	fullness	further

furtherance	fuse	fuselage
furthermore	fusibility	futile
furthest	fusible	futility
furtive	fusion	future
fury	infuse	futurist
furious	transfuse	futurity

G

gable	gangway	gastronomic
gage	gap	gate
gain	garage	gatehouse
gained	garb	gatekeeper
gainful	garbage	gatepost
gainsay	garble	gateway
galaxy	gardener	gather
gall	gargoyle	gathered
gallant	garland	gatherer
gallantry	garlic	gaudy
gallery	garment	gauge
gallon	garner	gauger
gallop	garnet	gauntlet
galvanize	garnish	gauze
galvanism	garnishee	gay
galvanization	garnisher	gayety
gambit	garnishment	gayly
gamble	garniture	gayness
gambled	garrison	gazelle
gambler	garrulous	gazette
gamut	garrulity	gelatin
ganglion	garter	gelatinize
gangrene	gasoline	gelatinoid
gangrenous	gasp	gelatinous
	gastric	gender

genealogy	genteel	gerund
general	gentian	gerundive
generalissimo	Gentile	gesso
generality	gentle	gesticulate
generalization	gentility	gesture
generalize	gentleman	geyser
generally	gentlemen	ghastly
generalship	gentleness	ghost
generate	gently	ghostly
generated	gentry	giant
generates	genuflect	gift
generation	genuflection	gifted
generative	genuine	gigantic
generator	genuineness	gild
progenitor	genus	gilded
regenerate	geodetic	gilder
generic	geography	gill
generous	geology	gimlet
generosity	geometry	ginger
genesis	germ	giraffe
genial	germicide	gird
congenial	germinal	girder
geniality	germinate	girdle
genially	germination	girl
genitive	germinative	girlhood

girlish	glide	gluttonous
girth	glided	gnarled
give	glider	gnat
forgive	glimpse	gnaw
gave	glissando	gneiss
given	glisten	gnome
giver	glistened	gnomon
glacier	globe	gnu
glacial	globular	go
glad	globule	gocart
gladden	gloom	gone
gladdened	gloomily	goat
gladly	gloominess	gobble
gladness	glory	goblet
gladsome	glories	God
gladiator	glorification	godchild
gladiatorial	glorify	goddess
gladiolus	glorious	godfather
glamour	inglorious	godhead
glamorous	glossary	godhood
glass	glossiness	godless
glassful	glove	godlike
glassiness	glucose	godling
glazier	glue	godly
gleeful	glutton	godparent

godsend	gossip	graduation
goggle	gouache	undergraduate
goiter	gouge	grain
gold	gourd	granary
golden	govern	grammar
goldenrod	governable	grammarian
goldfish	governess	grammatical
goldsmith	government	grand
golf	governmental	aggrandize
golfer	governor	grandchild
gondola	misgovern	grandeur
gondolier	ungovernable	grandfather
good	grace	grandiloquence
good-by	graceful	grandiloquent
goodliness	graceless	grandiose
goodly	gracious	grandly
goodness	grade	grandness
goose	degrade	grandparent
gooseberry	gradation	granite
gopher	gradient	grant
gorge	ungraded	granulate
gorgeous	gradual	granule
gorilla	gradually	grape
gospel	graduate	grapefruit
gossamer	graduated	grapeshot

grapevine	greasiness	grimy
graphic	great	grind
graphical	greater	grinder
graphics	greatest	grindstone
graphophone	greatly	groaned
grapple	greatness	grocer
grasshopper	greed	grocery
grateful	greedier	groom
gratification	greediest	groomed
gratify	greedily	grotesque
gratis	greediness	ground
gratitude	green	background
gratuitous	greener	foreground
gratuity	greenery	groundless
ingrate	greenhorn	groundwork
ingratitude	greenhouse	underground
ungrateful	greenish	group
gravamen	greenroom	grovel
gravel	gregarious	grow
gravitate	Gregorian	grower
gravitation	gridiron	grown
gravity	grief	growl
grease	grievance	grub
greasewood	grievous	grudge
greasily	grimace	gruel

gruesome	beguile	gunpowder
gruff	guillotine	gunshot
grumble	guilt	gunsmith
grunt	guiltily	gunstock
guarantee	guiltiness	gunwale
guaranteed	guiltless	gurgle
guarantor	guilty	gush
guard	guinea	gusher
guarded	guise	gusset
guardian	guitar	gust
guardsman	gullet	gusto
guava	gullible	gutter
gubernatorial	gulp	guttural
guerdon	gum	gymnasium
guerrilla	gun	gymnast
guide	gunboat	gymnastic
guidance	guncotton	gypsum
guidebook	gunfire	gypsy
guided	gunman	gyrate
guild	gunner	gyratory
guile	gunnery	gyroscope

H

haberdasher	halberd	handspring
haberdashery	halibut	handwriting
habit	Halloween	longhand
habitable	hallucination	shorthand
habitant	hallucinatory	handle
habitat	halogen	handlebar
habitation	halter	handsome
habitual	hammer	hang
habituate	hammerless	hanger
habituated	hammock	hangman
habitude	hamper	hanker
habitué	hampered	hansom
hackman	unhampered	haphazard
hackneyed	hand	hapless
hacksaw	handball	happen
haddock	handbook	happened
haggle	handcuff	happy
hailstone	handful	happily
hair	handicap	happiness
hairbreadth	handicraft	unhappy
hairbrush	handily	harangue
hairdresser	handiness	harass
hairpin	handiwork	harbinger
hairspring	handkerchief	harbor
	handmade	hard

harden	harmonize	hatchet
hardened	harness	hatchway
hardener	harp	hate
hard-fisted	harpist	hated
hard-headed	harpoon	hateful
hard-hearted	harpsichord	hatefully
hardihood	harrier	hatefulness
hardiness	harsh	hatred
hardness	harsher	haughty
hardpan	harshest	haul
hard-shell	harshly	haulage
hardship	harshness	hauled
hardware	hartshorn	haunt
unhardened	harvest	haunted
harelip	harvester	have
Harlequin	harvests	havoc
harm	hash	hawk
harmful	hassock	hawker
harmless	haste	hawk-eyed
unharmed	hasten	hawkweed
harmony	hastened	hay
harmonic	hastily	haycock
harmonica	hastiness	hayloft
harmonious	hatch	haymow
harmonization	hatchery	hayrack

hayseed	headsman	heartbeat
haystack	headstone	heartbreak
hazard	headstrong	heartbroken
haphazard	headwater	heartburn
hazardous	headway	heartened
haze	headwork	heartfelt
hazily	heal	heartily
haziness	healed	heartless
hazel	healer	heart-rending
head	health	hearth
headache	healthful	hearthstone
headband	healthfulness	heater
headboard	healthily	heath
headdress	unhealed	heathen
headed	unhealthy	heathenish
headfirst	hear	heathenism
headgear	heard	heather
headily	hearer	heaven
headland	hearsay	heavenly
headless	unheard	heavenward
headlight	hearken	heavy
headline	hearse	heavier
headlong	heart	heaviest
headpiece	downhearted	heavily
headquarters	heartache	heaviness

hecatomb	helix	herald
heckle	heliograph	heraldic
hectic	heliotrope	heraldry
hectograph	helium	herb
hedge	help	herbaceous
hedgehog	helped	herbage
hedgerow	helper	herbal
hedonism	helpfully	herbarium
heed	helpfulness	herbivorous
heeded	helpless	Herculean
heedfully	helpmate	here
heedfulness	hematite	hereabouts
heedless	hemicycle	hereafter
heedlessness	hemisphere	hereat
hegemony	hemlock	hereby
hegira	hemorrhage	hereinafter
heifer	hemstitch	hereinbefore
height	hence	hereof
heighten	henceforth	hereto
heinous	henceforward	heretofore
heir	henequen	hereunto
heiress	hepatica	hereupon
heirloom	heptagon	herewith
helical	heptameter	heredity
helicoid	heptangular	hereditability

hereditable		unhesitating		highlander	
hereditament		heterogeneous		highly	
hereditary		heterogeneity		high-minded	
heritability		homogeneous		highness	
heritable		hexagon		high-pressure	
heritage		hexagonal		highroad	
inherit		hexameter		highway	
heresy		hexangular		highwayman	
heretic		hexapod		hike	
hermetic		hiatus		hilarious	
hermit		hibernate		hilarity	
hermitage		hibernation		hill	
hero		hickory		hilliness	
heroic		hide		hillock	
heroical		hidden		hillside	
heroine		hideous		hilltop	
heroism		hierarchy		hilt	
heron		hieratic		himself	
herring		high		hinder	
herself		height		hindrance	
hesitate		heighten		hinge	
hesitance		highborn		hint	
hesitancy		highboy		hinted	
hesitant		high-handed		hippodrome	
hesitation		highland		hippopotamus	

hire	hollow	homonym
hireling	holy	homunculus
hirsute	holily	honest
his	holiness	dishonest
hiss	unholy	honestly
histology	homage	honesty
history	home	honey
historian	homeless	honeybee
historic	homelike	honeycomb
historical	homeliness	honeyed
histrionic	homesickness	honeymoon
hitch	homespun	honeysuckle
hither	homestead	honor
hitherto	homeward	dishonor
hive	homeopathy	honorable
hoard	Homeric	honorarium
hobble	homicide	honorary
hog	homicidal	unhonored
hogback	homily	hood
hogfish	homiletics	hooded
hoggish	hominy	hoodwink
hogshead	homogeneous	hookworm
hogweed	heterogeneous	hope
hoist	homogeneity	hopefully
holiday	homologous	hopefulness

hopelessly	horsewoman	houses
unhoped	unhorsed	housewarming
hopscotch	hortatory	housewife
horizon	horticulture	housework
horizontal	hosier	ice house
horizontally	hosiery	storehouse
horned	hospital	warehouse
hornet	hospitality	hovel
horoscope	hostage	hover
horror	hostile	how
horrible	hostilely	anyhow
horrid	hostility	however
horrify	hot	howsoever
horse	hot-headed	somehow
horseback	hothouse	howitzer
horse-chestnut	hotness	hubbub
horseflesh	hound	huckleberry
horsefly	hour	huckster
horsehair	hourglass	huge
horsehide	hourly	Huguenot
horseman	house	hulk
horsepower	household	human
horse-radish	householder	humane
horseshoe	housekeeper	humaneness
horsewhip	housemaid	humanism

humanitarian		hundredth		huskiness	
humanity		hunger		hussar	
humanization		hungered		hustings	
humanize		hungrily		hustle	
humankind		hunk		hustled	
humble		hunt		hustler	
humbleness		hunted		hutch	
humblest		hunter		hyacinth	
humbug		huntsman		hyaline	
humdrum		hurdle		hybrid	
humid		hurdled		hydrant	
humidify		hurdler		hydrate	
humidity		hurl		hydraulic	
humidor		hurricane		hydrocarbon	
humiliate		hurry		hydrochloric	
humiliation		unhurried		hydroelectric	
humility		hurt		hydrogen	
hummock		hurtful		hydrometer	
humor		hurtfulness		hydrophobia	
humorist		unhurt		hydroplane	
humorous		husband		hydrostatics	
humorousness		husbandry		hydroxide	
hunch		husbands		hygiene	
hundred		husk		hygienic	
hundredfold		huskily		hygienically	

hymnal	hypnosis	hypocritical
hyperbola	hypnotic	hypodermic
hyperbole	hypnotism	hypotenuse
hypercritical	hypnotist	hypothecate
hypertrophy	hypnotize	hypothesis
hyphen	hypochondria	hypothetical
hyphenate	hypochondriac	hysteria
hyphenated	hypocrisy	hysterical
hyphened	hypocrite	hysterics

I

iambic
ibex
ibis
ice
  iceberg
  icebound
  ice house
  iceman
  icicle
  icily
  iciness
ichor
ichthyology
icon
  iconoclasm
  iconoclast
idea
  ideas
ideal
  idealism
  idealist
  idealistic
  ideality
  idealization

idealize
ideally
identic
  identical
  identification
  identify
  identity
  unidentified
idiocy
  idiot
  idiotic
idiom
  idiomatic
  unidiomatic
idiosyncrasy
idle
  idled
  idleness
  idler
  idly
idol
  idolater
  idolatry
  idolize
idyl

idyllic
igneous
ignite
  ignites
  ignition
ignoble
ignominy
  ignominious
ignorance
  ignorant
  ignorantly
ignore
iguana
ilk
illegal
  illegality
illegible
illegitimate
illiberal
illicit
illiterate
  illiteracy
illness
illogical
illuminate

illuminant	imitate	immobilization
illumination	imitable	immobilize
illuminator	imitation	immoderate
illumine	imitative	immodest
illusion	imitator	immolate
illusive	inimitable	immoral
illusory	immaculate	immorality
illustrate	immaculately	immortal
illustration	immanent	immortality
illustrative	immaterial	immortalize
illustrator	immature	immortally
illustrious	immeasurable	immovable
image	immediate	immune
imagery	immediately	immunity
imagine	immediateness	immunize
imaginable	immemorial	immunology
imaginary	immense	immure
imagination	immensely	immutable
imaginative	immerse	immutability
unimaginable	immersion	imp
imbecile	immigrant	impish
imbecility	immigration	impact
imbibe	imminent	impair
imbroglio	imminence	impaired
imbue	immobile	impairment

unimpaired	impedance	impersonate
impale	impediment	impersonation
impalpable	impedimenta	impersonator
impalpability	impel	impertinent
impanel	impend	impertinence
impart	impenetrable	imperturbable
impartial	impenetrability	imperturbability
impartiality	impenitent	impervious
impartially	impenitence	impetuous
impassion	imperative	impetuosity
impassionate	imperceptible	impetus
impassioned	imperfect	impinge
impassive	imperfection	impious
impassivity	imperfectly	impiety
impatient	imperforate	implacable
impatience	imperial	implacability
impeach	imperialism	implant
impeachable	imperialist	implement
impeachment	imperialistic	implicate
unimpeachable	imperially	implication
impeccable	imperious	implicit
impeccability	imperil	implore
impecunious	imperiled	imply
impecuniosity	imperishable	implied
impede	impersonal	impolite

impolitely	impracticable	improper
impolitic	impracticability	impropriety
imponderable	imprecate	improve
import	imprecation	improvable
importable	imprecatory	improvement
importance	impregnable	unimproved
important	impregnability	improvident
importation	impregnate	improvise
imported	impregnation	improvisation
importer	impresario	imprudent
unimportant	imprescriptible	imprudence
importune	impress	impudent
importunacy	impression	impudence
importunate	impressionable	impugn
importunity	impressionism	impugnable
impose	impressionistic	impugned
imposition	impressive	impugnment
impossible	imprimatur	impulse
impossibility	imprint	impulsion
impost	imprison	impulsive
impostor	imprisoned	impunity
imposture	imprisonment	impure
impotent	improbable	impurely
impoverish	improbability	impurity
impoverishment	impromptu	impute

imputable

imputation

imputative

inability

  unable

inaccessible

  inaccessibility

inaccurate

  inaccuracy

inaction

  inactive

  inactivity

inadequate

  inadequacy

inadmissible

inadvertent

inadvisable

  inadvisability

inalienable

inane

  inanity

inanimate

inanition

inapplicable

inapposite

inappreciable

  inappreciative

  inappropriate

inapt

  inaptitude

inarticulate

inartistic

inasmuch

inattention

  attention

  attentive

  inattentive

inaudible

inaugurate

  inaugural

  inauguration

inauspicious

inborn

incalculable

incandesce

  incandescence

  incandescent

incantation

incapable

incapacitate

incapacitation

incarcerate

incarnate

incarnation

incendiary

incense

incentive

inception

incertitude

incessant

inch

inchoate

incident

  incidence

  incidental

  incidentally

incinerate

incineration

incinerator

incipient

incise

incised

incision

incisive

incisor

incite

incitement

incivility

inclement

clement

inclemency

incline

decline

inclination

inclined

recline

inclose

inclosure

include

included

inclusion

inclusive

incognito

incoherent

incoherence

incombustible

income

incommensurate

incomparable

incompatible

incompatibility

incompetent

incompetence

incomplete

incomprehensible

incomprehensibility

inconclusive

incongruous

incongruity

inconsequential

inconsiderate

inconsiderable

inconsistent

inconsistency

inconsolable

inconspicuous

inconspicuously

inconstancy

incontestable

incontrovertible

inconvenient

inconvenience

incorporate

incorporation

incorporator

incorrect

incorrigible

incorrigibility

incorruptible

incorruptibility

increase

increased

incredible

incredibility

incredulity

incredulous

increment

incriminate

incrimination

incriminatory

incubate

incubation

incubator

incubus

inculcate

inculcation

inculpate

inculpation

inculpatory

incumbent

incunabula	indented	indifferent
incur	indention	indifferently
incurable	indenture	indigenous
indebtedness	independent	indigent
indecent	independence	indigence
indecency	indescribable	indigestion
indecision	indestructible	indigestible
indecisive	indeterminate	indignant
indecorous	indeterminable	indignation
indecorum	index	indignity
indeed	indexer	indigo
indefatigable	indexes	indirect
indefensible	indices	indirection
indefinable	Indian	indirectness
indefinite	indicate	indiscreet
indefiniteness	contraindicate	indiscretion
indelible	indication	indiscriminate
indelibility	indicative	indispensable
indelicate	indicator	indispose
indelicacy	indicatory	indisposition
indemnify	indicia	indisputable
indemnification	indict	indissoluble
indemnity	indictable	indistinct
indent	indictment	indistinctly
indentation	indifference	indistinctness

indistinguishable
indite
individual
individualism
individualist
individualistic
individuality
individualize
indivisible
indolent
indolence
indomitable
indoors
indorse
indorsed
indorsee
indorsement
indorser
indorses
unindorsed
indubitable
induce
inducement
induct
inductance

induction
inductive
inductor
indulge
indulgence
indulgent
industry
industrial
industrialism
industrialist
industrialize
industrially
industrious
inebriate
inebriation
inebriety
inedible
ineffable
ineffective
ineffectual
ineffectually
inefficient
inefficiency
inelegance
inelegant

ineligible
ineluctable
inept
ineptitude
inequality
inequitable
ineradicable
inerrant
inert
inertia
inertness
inestimable
inevitable
inevitability
inexact
inexactitude
inexcusable
inexhaustible
inexhaustibility
inexhaustibly
inexorable
inexpedient
inexpensive
inexperience
inexplicable

inextricable	infernal	inflection
inextricability	inferno	inflexible
infallible	infertile	inflexibility
infallibility	infertility	inflict
infamy	infest	infliction
infamous	infidel	influence
infant	infidelity	influential
infancy	infiltrate	uninfluenced
infanticide	infinite	influenza
infantile	infinitesimal	influx
infantry	infinitive	efflux
infatuate	infinitude	inform
infatuated	infinity	informal
infatuation	infirm	informality
infeasible	infirmary	informant
infect	infirmity	information
infection	inflame.	informative
infectious	inflammability	informer
infelicitous	inflammable	misinform
infelicity	inflammation	uninformed
infer	inflammatory	infraction
inference	inflate	infrangible
inferential	inflated	infrequent
inferior	inflation	infringe
inferiority	inflect	infringement

infuriate	inhabited	inhumanity
infuriated	uninhabited	inimical
infuse	inhale	inimitable
infusible	inhalation	iniquity
infusion	inhaled	iniquitous
ingenious	inhaler	initial
ingenuity	inharmonious	initially
ingenuous	inhere	initiate
ingest	inhered	initiation
ingestion	inherence	initiatory
inglorious	inherent	uninitiated
ingot	inherit	inject
ingrain	disinherit	injection
ingrained	hereditary	injector
ingratiate	heritage	injudicious
ingratiation	inheritable	injunction
ingratiatory	inheritance	injure
ingredient	inherited	injured
ingress	inheritor	injuries
ingrown	inhibit	injurious
inhabit	inhibition	injury
inhabitable	inhibitory	uninjured
inhabitancy	inhospitable	injustice
inhabitant	inhuman	unjust
inhabitation	inhumane	ink

inkhorn	innumerable	inscriber
inkling	inoculate	inscription
inkstand	inoffensive	inscrutable
inkwell	inoperable	inscrutability
inky	inoperative	insect
inlaid	inopportune	insecticide
inland	inopportuneness	insectivorous
inlet	inordinate	insecure
inmate	coordinate	insecurity
inmost	subordinate	insensible
inn	inorganic	insensate
innate	inpatient	insensibility
inner	inquest	insensitive
innermost	inquietude	insentience
inning	inquire	insentient
innocence	inquirer	inseparable
innocent	inquires	insert
innocently	inquiries	inserted
innocents	inquiry	insertion
innocuous	inquisition	inset
innovate	inquisitive	inshore
innovation	insane	inside
innovative	insanity	insider
innovator	insanitary	insidious
innuendo	inscribe	insight

insignia	inspire	institutional
insignificant	inspiration	instruct
insignificance	inspirational	instruction
insincere	inspired	instructional
insincerely	inspirer	instructive
insincerity	inspires	instructor
insinuate	instability	instructress
insinuated	install	uninstructed
insinuation	installation	instrument
insipid	installed	instrumental
insipidity	installment	instrumentalist
insist	instant	instrumentality
insistence	instance	instrumentally
insistent	instantaneous	instrumentation
insobriety	instantly	insubordinate
insolent	instead	insubordination
insolence	instep	insufferable
insoluble	instigate	insufficient
insolvency	instigation	insulate
insolvent	instigator	insular
insomnia	instill	insularity
insomuch	instinct	insulation
inspect	instinctive	insulator
inspection	institute	uninsulated
inspector	institution	insult

insults	integument	intentness
insuperable	intellect	unintentional
insuperability	intellectual	interborough
insupportable	intellectually	intercede
insuppressible	intelligent	interceded
insure	intelligence	intercession
insurability	intelligibility	intercept
insurable	intelligible	interception
insurance	unintelligent	interchangeable
uninsured	intemperate	intercollegiate
insurgent	intemperance	intercourse
insurmountable	intemperately	interdenom- inational
insurrection	intend	interdependent
insurrectionary	intent	interdict
intact	intention	interdiction
intaglio	intendant	interest
intake	intense	interested
intangible	intensification	uninterested
intangibility	intensify	interfere
integer	intensity	interference
disintegrate	intensive	interim
integral	intent	interior
integrate	intend	interject
integration	intention	interlock
integrity	intentional	interlocutor

interloper

interlude

intermarriage

intermediate

intermediary

intermezzo

interminable

intermingle

intermit

intermission

intermittence

intermittent

intermixture

intern

internment

internal

internally

international

internecine

interpellate

interpellation

interpolate

interpolation

interpose

interposition

interpret

interpretation

interpretative

interpreter

interregnum

interrelation

interrogate

interrogation

interrogative

interrogatory

interrupt

interrupted

interruption

uninterrupted

interscholastic

intersect

intersperse

interstate

interstice

interstices

interstitial

intertwine

intertwined

interval

intervene

intervention

non-intervention

interview

interweave

intestate

intestine

intimate

intimacy

intimated

intimation

intimidate

intimidated

intimidation

into

intolerance

intolerable

intolerant

intone

intonation

intoxicate

intoxicant

intoxicated

intoxication

non-intoxicating

intractable

intransigent
  intransigence
intransitive
intrastate
intrenchment
intrepid
  intrepidity
intricate
  extricate
  intricacy
intrigue
intrinsic
  extrinsic
introduce
  introduction
  introductory
introit
introspect
  introspection
  introspective
introvert
  introversion
intrude
  intruder
  intrusion

intrusive
intrust
intuition
  intuitive
inunction
inundate
  inundation
inure
invade
  invasion
invalid
  invalidate
  invalidation
  invalidity
invaluable
invar
  invariable
  invariability
inveigh
  invective
inveigle
invent
  invention
  inventive
  inventor

inventory
inverse
  inversion
  invert
  inverted
invest
  invested
  investment
  investor
  invests
  reinvest
investigate
  investigation
  investigative
  investigator
inveterate
invidious
invigorate
  invigoration
invincible
  invincibility
inviolable
  inviolability
  inviolate
invisible

invisibility	ionize	irrationally
invite	Ionic	irreclaimable
invitation	iota	irreconcilable
uninvited	ipecac	irrecoverable
invoice	irate	irredeemable
invoices	irascibility	irrefragable
invoke	irascible	irrefrangible
invocation	iris	irrefutable
involuntary	iridescence	irregular
involuntarily	iridescent	irregularity
involute	iridium	irrelevant
involution	irk	irreligious
involve	irksome	irremediable
invulnerable	iron	irremovable
invulnerability	flatiron	irreparable
inward	ironclad	irreplaceable
inwardly	ironside	irrepressible
inwardness	ironware	irreproachable
iodine	ironwood	irresistible
iodate	ironwork	irresistibility
iodic	irony	irresoluble
iodide	ironical	irresolute
iodize	irradiate	irresolution
ion	irradiation	irrespective
ionization	irrational	irresponsible

irresponsibility	irritative	isthmus
irretraceable	irruption	Italy
irretrievable	isinglass	Italian
irreverent	Islam	itchy
irreverence	island	item
irreversible	isobar	itemize
irrevocable	isolate	itinerate
irrigate	isolation	itinerancy
irrigation	isomeric	itinerant
irritate	isotherm	itinerary
irritability	issue	its
irritable	issuance	itself
irritant	reissue	ivory
irritation	unissued	ivy

J

jackal	jewelry	jollity
Jacobean	Jewish	jonquil
jaguar	jingle	jostle
janitor	jingo	jot
January	jingoism	jounce
japan	jinrikisha	journal
jargon	jinx	journalism
jasmine	jitney	journalist
jaundice	jockey	journalize
jauntily	jocose	journey
jealous	jocosity	jovial
Jehovah	jocular	joviality
jejune	jocularity	jowl
jellyfish	jocund	joy
jeopardy	jocundity	enjoy
jeopardize	join	joyful
jerk	adjoin	joyless
jerkily	disjoin	joyous
jersey	enjoin	jubilate
Jesus	jointed	jubilance
Jesuit	jointure	jubilant
jetsam	joist	jubilation
jettison	joker	jubilee
jewel	jolly	judge
	jollification	adjudge

judged	junction	injustice
judgeship	juncture	justice
judgment	jungle	justiciar
judicial	junior	justifiable
judicative	juniper	justification
judicatory	junk	justificatory
judicature	jurist	justify
judicially	juridical	justly
judiciary	jurisdiction	justness
judicious	jurisprudence	unjust
juggle	juror	unjustifiable
jugular	jury	juvenile
jumble	juryman	juvenility
jump	just	juxtaposition

K

kaiser	kind	kith
kaleidoscope	kinder	kitten
kaleidoscopic	kindest	kleptomaniac
kangaroo	kindliness	knave
kaolin	kindly	knavery
keep	kindness	knavish
bookkeeper	kinds	kneecap
housekeeper	unkind	knight
keeper	kindergarten	knighted
keepsake	kindred	knights
kept	kine	unknightly
timekeeper	kinetic	knot
kennel	king	knotted
kernel	kingbird	unknotted
kerosene	kingbolt	know
kersey	kingcraft	knew
keyboard	kingdom	knowable
khedive	kingfisher	knowingness
kidnap	kinglet	knowledge
kidney	kingliness	known
kiln	king-pin	unknown
kilogram	kingship	knuckle
kilometer	kinsman	knurl
kilt	kiosk	kopeck
	kitchen	krypton

L

label	ladylike	landholder
labial	ladyship	landlady
labor	laggard	landlocked
laboratory	lagoon	landlord
labored	laity	landmark
laborer	lambent	landowner
laborious	lame	landscape
laburnum	lamed	landslip
labyrinth	lamely	landsman
lacerate	lameness	landward
lacerated	lament	language
laceration	lamentable	languid
lachrymal	lamentation	languish
lachrymose	lamented	languor
lacquer	lamina	languorous
lacrosse	laminate	lantern
lactic	laminated	lanthanum
lacuna	lamination	lanyard
lacunae	lampoon	lapel
lacunas	lamprey	lapidary
ladder	lancet	lapse
laden	lancination	larboard
ladle	land	larceny
lady	landed	larcenous
	landfall	larch

lard	later	laugh
large	latest	laughable
enlarge	latter	laughingstock
largely	latent	laughter
larger	lateral	launch
largest	laterally	launder
lariat	lath	laundress
lark	lathe	laundry
larkspur	lather	laundryman
larva	Latin	laurel
larval	Latinism	laureate
larynx	Latinist	lava
laryngitis	Latinity	lavaliere
lassitude	latitude	lavatory
lasso	latitudinal	lavender
last	latter	lavish
lasted	lattermost	law
lastly	lattice	lawful
lasts	latticework	lawgiver
latch	laud	lawless
latchkey	laudability	lawmaker
latchstring	laudable	lawsuit
late	laudation	lawyer
lately	laudatory	lax
lateness	laudanum	laxative

laxity	leather	legation
laxness	leatheret	legato
relax	leathern	legend
layer	leatheroid	legendary
lazy	leatherwood	legerdemain
lazily	leathery	legging
laziness	leaven	legible
lead	lectern	illegible
leaden	lecture	legibility
leader	lecturer	legion
leadership	ledger	legionary
leadsman	leeward	legislate
league	leeway	legislation
leak	left	legislative
leakage	left-handed	legislator
leakiness	legacy	legislature
learn	legal	legitimate
learned	illegal	illegitimate
learnt	legalism	legitimacy
lease	legality	legitimateness
leasehold	legalization	legitimation
leaseholder	legalize	legitimatize
lessee	legally	legitimist
lessor	legate	legume
least	legatee	leguminous

leisure	leprosy	leverage
leisureliness	leprous	leviathan
leisurely	lesion	levitate
lemon	less	levitation
lemonade	least	levity
lemur	lessen	lexicon
length	lessened	lexicography
lengthen	lesser	liable
lengthily	lesson	liability
lengthiness	let	liaison
lengthways	lethal	liar
lengthwise	lethargy	libation
lengthy	lethargic	libel
lenient	lethargical	libelant
lenience	letter	libeled
leniently	lettered	libelee
lenitive	letterhead	libeler
lenity	letterpress	libelous
Lent	lettuce	liberal
Lenten	levant	illiberal
lentil	levee	liberalism
lenticular	level	liberality
leonine	leveled	liberalization
leopard	leveler	liberalizer
leper	lever	liberally

liberty	lift	lignite
liberate	ligate	like
liberated	ligament	dislike
liberation	ligation	likable
liberator	ligature	likelihood
library	light	likely
librarian	alight	liken
libretto	delightful	likened
license	enlightenment	likeness
licensed	lighted	likes
licensee	lighten	likewise
licentiate	lightened	unlikely
lichen	lighter	lilac
licorice	lightest	lilt
lictor	lighthouse	lily
liege	lightly	limber
lien	light-minded	lime
lieu	lightness	limekiln
lieutenant	lightning	limelight
life	lights	limewater
lifeless	lightship	limit
lifelike	lightsome	limitable
lifelong	relight	limitation
lifetime	ligneous	limited
lives	lignify	limitless

limousine		linotype		listener	
limpid		lintel		liter	
limpidity		lion		literate	
linden		lioness		illiterate	
line		lionize		literacy	
align		liquid		literal	
lineage		liquefaction		literalism	
lineal		liquefiable		literality	
lineament		liquefy		literalize	
linear		liquescent		literary	
lined		liquidate		literature	
lineman		liquidation		transliterate	
liner		liquidator		litharge	
reline		liquidity		lithe	
unlined		liquor		lithesome	
linen		lira		lithia	
linger		lire		lithium	
lingerie		lissom		lithograph	
lingual		list		litigate	
linguist		enlist		litigable	
linguistic		listless		litigant	
linguistics		lists		litigation	
liniment		reenlist		litigious	
linkage		listen		litmus	
linoleum		listened		litter	

little	localism	loftiness
littoral	locality	logarithm
liturgy	localization	loggia
liturgic	localize	logic
live	locally	illogical
live	locate	logical
lived	allocate	logician
livelihood	dislocate	logotype
liveliness	location	logwood
livelong	lock	loiter
liver	locker	loitered
livery	locket	loiterer
livid	lockjaw	lone
lizard	lockout	loneliness
loaf	locksmith	lonesome
loaves	locomotion	lonesomeness
loam	locomotive	long
loathe	locus	belong
loathful	loci	elongate
loathly	locust	longboat
loathsome	lodge	longed
lobby	lodger	longer
lobbyist	lodgment	longest
lobster	loft	longevity
local	loftily	longhand

longhorn	lotus	low-spirited
longitude	loud	loyal
longitudinal	louder	loyalist
longshoreman	loudest	loyalty
prolong	loudly	lubricate
look	loudness	lubricant
outlook	lounge	lubrication
loop	love	lubricator
loophole	lovable	lucent
loose	loveless	lucid
loosen	loveliness	lucidity
loosened	lovely	luck
looseness	lover	luckily
loquacious	lovesick	luckiness
loquacity	unlovable	luckless
lord	low	lucrative
lordliness	lowborn	lucubration
lordship	lowboy	ludicrous
lore	lower	luggage
lorgnette	lowermost	lugubrious
lose	lowest	lukewarm
losable	lowland	lumbago
loss	lowliness	lumber
lost	lowness	luminous
lottery	low-pressure	luminary

luminescent	lurid	luxuriate
luminosity	lurk	luxurious
lump	luscious	lyceum
lunar	luster	lymphatic
lunacy	lustrous	lynx
lunatic	lute	lyonnaise
lunch	Lutheran	lyre
luncheon	luxury	lyric
lurch	luxuriance	lyrical
lure	luxuriant	lyricism

M

macabre	madrigal	magnificence
macadam	magazine	magnifico
macadamize	magenta	magnify
macaroni	maggot	magnification
macaroon	Magi	magnifier
macerate	magic	magniloquent
maceration	magician	magnitude
machete	magistrate	magnolia
machicolation	magisterial	magpie
machination	magistracy	maharaja
machine	magistral	mahogany
machinery	magistrature	maid
machinist	magnanimous	maiden
mackerel	magnanimity	maidenhair
macrocosm	magnate	maidenhood
microcosm	magnesium	maidenly
macron	magnesia	mail
maculate	magnet	mailable
immaculate	magnetic	mailed
mad	magnetically	mailer
madhouse	magnetism	unmailable
madman	magnetization	maim
madness	magnetize	maimed
madam	magneto	main
	magnificent	mainland

mainly	malapropos	malnutrition
mainmast	malaria	malodorous
mainsail	malarial	malpractice
mainspring	malassimilation	malt
mainstay	malcontent	Maltese
maintain	male	maltreat
maintainable	female	malversation
maintained	malediction	mammoth
maintenance	maledictory	man
majesty	malefactor	manhole
majestic	maleficent	manhood
majolica	malevolent	mankind
major	malfeasance	manly
majority	malformation	manslaughter
make	malice	men
make-believe	malicious	unmanned
maker	malign	manacle
makeshift	malignancy	manage
make-up	malignant	manageability
unmake	malignity	manageable
maladjustment	malignly	management
maladministration	malinger	manager
maladroit	malingerer	managerial
malady	malleable	managerially
malapert	malleability	managership

unmanageable	manner	marconigram
manatee	mannerism	mare
mandamus	mannerless	margin
mandarin	mannerly	marginal
mandate	unmannerly	marginalia
mandatory	manor	marginally
mandible	manorial	margrave
mandolin	mansion	marigold
maneuver	mantelpiece	marine
manganese	manual	mariner
manger	manually	submarine
mangy	manufacture	ultramarine
mania	manufactory	marionette
maniac	manufacturer	marital
maniacal	manumission	maritime
manicure	manure	mark
manicurist	manuscript	marked
manifest	many	markedly
manifestation	maple	marker
manifestly	maraschino	marksman
manifesto	maraud	unmarked
manifold	marauder	market
manifolder	marble	marketability
manikin	march	marketable
manipulate	marcher	marmalade

marmoset	masterful	materialization
maroon	masterliness	materialize
marooned	masterly	materially
marquis	masterpiece	maternal
marquise	masters	maternally
marry	mastership	maternity
marriage	masterwork	mathematics
marriageable	mastery	mathematician
unmarried	masthead	matinée
marshal	masticate	matricide
martial	mastication	matriculate
martially	mastiff	matrimony
martyr	mastodon	matrimonial
martyrdom	matador	matrimonially
marvel	match	matrix
marvelous	matchless	matrices
mascot	matchmaker	matron
masculine	matchwood	matter
masculinity	unmatched	mattress
mason	material	mature
masonry	immaterial	immature
massacre	materialism	maturity
massage	materialist	premature
massive	materialistic	maudlin
master	materiality	mausoleum

mauve	mechanical	meditate
maverick	mechanician	meditation
maxim	mechanism	meditative
maximum	mechanization	medium
mayhem	mechanize	media
mayonnaise	medal	mediums
mayor	medalist	meerschaum
mazurka	medallion	melancholy
meager	meddlesome	melancholia
mean	median	melancholic
meanly	mediate	meliorate
meanness	mediation	ameliorate
meantime	mediative	melioration
meanwhile	mediator	mellifluous
meander	medical	melodrama
measles	medicament	melodramatic
measure	medicate	melody
commensurate	medication	melodeon
measurably	medicative	melodic
measured	medicinal	melodious
measureless	medicine	melt
measurement	medieval	member
measurer	medievally	membership
measures	mediocre	memorandum
mechanic	mediocrity	memoranda

memorandums	mentality	meringue
memory	mentally	merino
commemorate	mention	merit
memento	mentioned	merited
memoir	mentor	meritorious
memorabilia	mephitic	unmerited
memorable	mercantile	mermaid
memorial	mercenary	merry
memorization	mercerize	merrily
memorize	merchant	merriment
menace	merchandise	merrymaking
menage	merchantman	mesa
menagerie	mercury	mesmerize
mendacious	mercurial	mesmerism
mendacity	mercy	mesquite
mendicant	merciful	message
mendicancy	merciless	messenger
menial	mere	metabolism
meningitis	merely	metal
meniscus	merest	metallic
mensuration	meretricious	metalloid
commensurate	merge	metallurgy
dimension	merger	metamorphose
mensurative	meridian	metamorphosis
mental	meridional	metaphor

metaphorical	macrocosm	militant
metaphysics	micrometer	militancy
metaphysical	microorganism	militarism
metaphysician	microphone	militarist
meteor	microscope	militaristic
meteoric	microscopic	military
meteorite	midnight	militate
meteorology	midst	militia
meter	midwinter	milk
method	might	milkman
methodical	almighty	milkweed
methodist	mightily	millennium
meticulous	mightiness	millenary
metric	mighty	millenial
metrical	migrate	milliner
metronome	migration	millinery
metropolis	migratory	million
metropolitan	mild	millionaire
mezzanine	mildly	millionth
miasma	mildness	mimeograph
miasmal	mildew	mimic
miasmatic	mile	mimicry
microbe	mileage	minaret
microbiology	milepost	minatory
microcosm	milestone	mind

mindful	miracle	miscellany
remind	miraculous	mischief
unmindful	mirage	mischievous
mined	mirror	misconception
mineral	mirth	misconduct
mineralogy	mirthful	misconstrue
mingle	mirthless	misconstruction
miniature	misadventure	miscount
minimize	misalliance	miscounted
minimization	misanthrope	miscreant
minimum	misanthropic	misdeed
minister	misanthropical	misdemeanor
administer	misapprehended	miser
ministerial	misapprehension	misery
ministration	misappropriate	miserable
ministry	misarrange	misfeasance
minor	misbehave	misfire
minster	misbehavior	misfit
minstrel	miscalculate	misfortune
mint	miscarry	misgiving
minuet	miscarries	misgovern
minus	miscegenation	mishap
minute	miscellaneous	misinform
minute	miscellanea	misinterpret
minutia	miscellanist	misjudged

misleading	mistook	moaned
mislike	mistreat	mobile
mismanage	mistress	immobile
misname	mistrial	mobility
misnomer	mistrust	mobilization
misplace	distrust	mobilize
misprint	mistrustful	moccasin
mispronounce	misunderstand	mock
misquote	misunderstood	mockery
misread	misuse	moderate
misrepresent	miter	immoderate
misrepresentation	mitered	moderately
misrule	mitigate	moderateness
missile	mitigable	moderation
mission	mitigation	moderator
missionary	mitten	modern
missive	mix	modernism
misspell	admixture	modernist
misspelled	miscible	modernity
misstate	mixed	modernization
misstatement	mixer	modernize
mistake	mixes	modest
mistakenly	mixture	modestly
unmistakable	mnemonic	modesty
mistletoe	moan	modicum

modify	momentarily	monogamous
modification	momentary	monogram
modifier	momently	monograph
modulate	momentous	monolith
mohair	momentum	monologue
Mohammedan	monarch	monologist
moist	anarchy	monomania
moisten	monarchial	monoplane
moistened	monarchism	monopoly
moistly	monarchist	monopolism
moisture	monarchy	monopolist
molasses	monastery	monopolistic
mold	monastic	monopolization
molecule	money	monopolize
molecular	monetary	monotone
molehill	monetize	monotonous
molest	moneyed	monotony
molestation	mongoose	monotype
unmolested	mongrel	monsoon
mollify	monitor	monster
mollification	monk	monstrosity
mollusk	monkey	monstrous
molten	monocle	month
molybdenum	monody	monthly
moment	monogamy	monument

monumental	furthermore	almost
mood	moreover	inmost
moodily	moribund	mostly
moodiness	morning	uppermost
moon	morocco	utmost
moonlight	moron	uttermost
moonshine	morose	motet
moonstone	morphine	mother
moral	morphology	godmother
demoralize	morsel	grandmother
immoral	mortal	motherhood
morale	immortalize	mother-in-law
moralism	mortality	motherland
moralist	mortally	motherless
moralistic	mortar	motherliness
morality	mortgage	mother-of-pearl
moralization	mortgagee	stepmother
moralize	mortgagor	motion
morally	mortify	motioned
moratorium	mortification	motionless
morbid	mortuary	motive
morbidity	mosaic	motivate
morbidly	mosquito	motivation
mordant	mossiness	motley
more	most	motor

motored	move	multiplex
motorist	immovable	multiplicand
motorman	movability	multiplication
motto	movable	multiplicative
mound	movement	multiplicity
mount	mover	multiplier
dismount	movie	multitude
mountain	remove	multitudinous
mountaineer	mower	mumble
mountainous	much	mummer
mounted	mucilage	mummery
remount	mucilaginous	mummy
surmount	mucous	mummification
unmounted	mulatto	mummify
mountebank	mulberry	mumps
mourn	mulct	mundane
mourner	mulcted	municipal
mournful	mule	municipality
mouse	multifarious	municipally
mice	multiform	munificent
mouser	multiformity	munificence
mouth	multigraph	munition
mouthed	multimillionaire	mural
mouthful	multiply	immure
mouthpiece	multiple	murder

murdered	musicale	mutilation
murderess	musician	mutilator
murderous	musket	mutiny
muriatic	musketeer	mutineer
murk	musketry	mutinous
murkily	muskmelon	mutton
murkiness	muskrat	mutual
murmur	muslin	mutually
murmurer	mussel	muzzle
murmurous	must	myopia
muscadine	mustache	myriad
muscatel	mustard	myrtle
muscle	muster	myself
muscular	mutate	mystery
muscularity	immutable	mysterious
muscularly	mutability	mystic
musculature	mutable	mystical
muse	mutation	mysticism
museum	mutative	mystification
mush	transmute	mystify
mushroom	mute	myth
music	muteness	mythical
musical	mutilate	mythology

N

nacre

nacreous

nainsook

naïve

naïveté

name

misnamed

namable

nameless

namely

names

namesake

nickname

surname

unnamed

napery

napkin

Napoleon

Napoleonic

narcissus

narcotic

narcosis

narcotism

narcotize

narrate

narration

narrative

narrator

narrow

narrowed

narrower

narrowest

narrowly

narrow-minded

narrowness

narwhal

nasal

nasality

nasalize

nasally

nascent

nasty

nastier

nastiest

nastily

nastiness

natation

nation

international

national

nationalism

nationalistic

nationality

nationalization

nationalize

nationally

native

nativity

nature

natural

naturalism

naturalist

naturalistic

naturalization

naturalize

naturally

naturalness

preternatural

supernatural

unnatural

naughty

naughtiest

naughtily

naughtiness

nausea	nebula	neediness
nauseate	nebulosity	needless
nauseous	nebulous	nefarious
nautical	necessary	negative
aeronautic	necessaries	negation
nautilus	necessarily	neglect
navigate	necessitate	neglectful
circumnavigate	necessitous	negligence
navigability	necessity	negligent
navigable	unnecessary	negligible
navigation	neck	negotiate
navigator	neckband	negotiability
navy	neckcloth	negotiable
naval	neckerchief	negotiation
near	necklace	negotiator
nearer	necktie	neighbor
nearest	neckwear	neighborhood
nearly	necrology	neighborly
nearness	necropolis	neither
nearsighted	necromancy	Nemesis
neat	nectar	neolithic
neater	need	neon
neatest	needed	neophyte
neatly	needful	nepenthe
neatness	needfully	nephew

nepotism

nerve

  nerveless

  nervous

  unnerved

nescient

nestle

nether

network

neural

  neuralgia

  neurasthenia

  neurosis

  neurotic

neuter

  neutral

  neutrality

  neutralization

  neutralize

  neutrally

never

  nevermore

  nevertheless

new

  newcomer

newer

newest

newly

newness

newsmonger

newspaper

renewable

New Year's

next

nibble

nice

  nicely

  niceness

  nicer

  nicest

  nicety

nickel

  nickeliferous

  nickelodeon

nickname

nicotine

niggard

night

  nightdress

  nightfall

nightgown

nightingale

nightly

nightmare

nights

nighttime

nihilism

  nihilist

  nihilistic

nimble

nimbus

niter

  nitrate

  nitric

  nitrification

  nitrify

  nitrogen

  nitrogenous

  nitroglycerin

  nitrous

noble

  ignoble

  nobility

  nobleman

  nobler

noblest	non-commissioned	noontide
nobody	noncommittal	noontime
nocturne	non-communicant	norm
nocturnal	non-conductor	abnormal
noise	non-conformity	normal
noiseless	non-conformist	normalcy
noisily	nondescript	normality
noisiness	none	normally
noisome	nonentity	subnormal
nomad	nonesuch	Norman
nomadic	non-existence	north
nomenclature	non-metallic	northeast
misnomer	nonpareil	northeaster
nominal	non-participating	northeasterly
nominally	non-payment	northeastern
nominate	nonplus	northeastward
denominate	non-resident	northerly
nomination	non-resistant	northern
nominee	nonsense	northerner
nonagenarian	nonsensical	northernmost
nonagon	non-subscriber	northland
non-appearance	non-suit	northwest
nonchalant	non-union	northwesterly
nonchalance	noon	northwestern
non-combatant	noonday	nose

noseband

nosebleed

nosegay

nostril

nostrum

not

note

annotate

connote

denote

notability

notable

notarial

notary

notation

notebook

noted

noteworthy

nothing

nothingness

notice

noticeable

notify

notification

notion

notorious

notoriety

notwithstanding

noun

pronoun

nourish

nourishment

novel

novelette

novelist

novelize

novelty

novice

novitiate

now

nowadays

nowhere

noxious

innoxious

obnoxious

nozzle

nucleate

nuclear

nucleation

nucleus

nude

nudity

nudge

nugatory

nugget

nuisance

null

nullification

nullify

nullity

numb

numbness

number

numberless

numeral

enumerate

innumerable

numerate

numeration

numerator

numerical

numerous

numismatics

nuncio

nunnery

nuptial	nursery	nutriment
nurse	nurseryman	nutrition
nursed	nurture	nutritious
nursemaid	nutmeg	nutritive

O

oat

oaten

oatmeal

oath

obbligato

obdurate

obduracy

obedient

disobedient

obedience

obeisance

obelisk

obese

obesity

obey

disobey

obituary

object

objectify

objection

objectionable

objective

objectivity

objector

unobjectionable

objurgate

oblation

oblige

disoblige

obligate

obligation

obligatory

oblique

obliquity

obliterate

obliteration

transliterate

oblivion

oblivious

oblong

obloquy

obnoxious

oboe

obscene

obscenity

obscure

obscureness

obscurity

obsequious

obsequy

observe

observable

observance

observant

observation

observatory

observer

unobservant

obsess

obsessed

obsession

obsidian

obsolete

obsolescence

obsolescent

obsoletely

obsoleteness

obstacle

obstinate

obstinacy

obstinately

obstreperous

obstruct

obstruction

obstructionist	occlude	octopus
obstructive	occlusion	ocular
obstructor	occult	oculist
unobstructed	occultation	odd
obtain	occultism	oddity
obtainable	occupy	oddness
obtained	occupancy	odium
unobtainable	occupant	odious
obtrude	occupation	odometer
obtruder	occupational	odor
obtrusion	preoccupied	deodorize
obtrusive	unoccupied	malodorous
unobtrusive	occur	odoriferous
obtuse	occurrence	odorless
obverse	ocean	odorous
obviate	oceanic	of
obviation	oceanography	off
obvious	ocher	offal
occasion	ochlocracy	offcast
occasional	octave	off-color
occasionally	octagon	offend
occasioned	octagonal	inoffensive
occident	octameter	offender
occidental	octangular	offense
occiput	octavo	offensive

offer	oldest	onward
office	old-fashioned	thereon
officeholder	oldish	one
officer	oldness	no one
offices	oleomargarine	oneness
official	olfactory	oneself
officially	oligarchy	one-sided
officiate	olive	only
officiation	omega	onomatopoeia
officious	omelet	onus
often	omen	onerous
oftener	ominous	onyx
oftentimes	omit	ooze
ohm	omission	opal
ohmmeter	omnibus	opalesce
oil	omnipotent	opalescence
oilcloth	omnipotence	opalescent
oiler	omnipresent	opaque
oilily	omniscient	opacity
oiliness	nescient	open
oilskin	omniscience	open-air
oilstone	prescient	opener
old	on	open-eyed
olden	onlooker	open-faced
older	onto	open-hearted

open-hearth	opportunism	optometrist
openly	opportunist	opulent
openness	opportunity	opulence
openwork	oppose	opus
reopen	opposes	opera
unopened	opposite	or
opera	opposition	oracle
operetta	unopposed	oracular
operate	oppress	oracularly
cooperate	oppression	oral
operable	oppressive	orally
operated	oppressor	orange
operates	opprobrious	orangeade
operation	opprobrium	oration
operative	optic	orator
operator	optical	oratorical
ophthalmology	optician	oratorio
opinion	optimism	oratory
opinionated	optimist	orb
opinionative	optimistic	orbit
opium	optimistical	orchard
opiate	optimum	orchestra
opossum	option	orchestral
opponent	optional	orchestrate
opportune	optometry	orchestration

orchid

ordain

 ordained

 ordination

ordeal

order

 disorder

 orderliness

 reorder

ordinal

ordinance

ordinary

 extraordinary

 ordinarily

ordinate

 coordinate

 inordinate

 subordinate

ordnance

organ

 organic

 organically

 organism

 organist

organize

disorganize

organization

reorganize

unorganized

orgy

orient

 oriental

 orientalism

 orientalist

 orientate

 orientation

orifice

origin

 original

 originality

 originally

 originate

 origination

 originative

 originator

oriole

Orion

ormolu

ornate

 ornament

ornamental

ornamentation

ornithology

orotund

orphan

 orphanage

 orphaned

 orphanhood

orthochromatic

orthodox

 unorthodox

orthoëpy

orthography

orthopedic

oscillate

 oscillation

 oscillator

 oscillatory

osculate

osier

osmium

osmosis

osprey

ossify

 osseous

ostentation	outgo	overbalance
ostensible	outgrowth	overboard
ostentatious	outlandish	overburden
osteopath	outlaw	overcapitalize
ostracize	outlet	overcharge
ostracism	outline	overcoat
ostrich	outlined	overcome
other	outlive	overdevelop
otherwise	outlook	overdo
otiose	outnumber	overdraft
otter	output	overdriven
ourselves	outrage	overdue
out	outreach	overexpose
outcast	outrigger	overflow
outclass	outside	overhand
outcome	outstanding	overhang
outcrop	outtalk	overhaul
outcry	outward	overhead
outdistance	outwear	overinfluence
outdoors	outwit	overlap
outer	oval	overlook
outermost	oven	overnight
outfield	over	overpower
outfit	overalls	overproduction
outgeneral	overawe	overreach

overrule	overtone	ownership
overrun	overture	oxalic
overseer	overturn	oxygen
overshadow	overweight	dioxide
overshoe	overwhelm	hydroxide
oversight	overwhelmed	monoxide
oversize	overwrought	oxide
oversubscribe	owl	oxidize
overt	owlet	oxyhydrogen
overtake	owlish	protoxide
overthrow	own	oyster
overtime	owner	ozone

P

pabulum	paid	palladium
pacemaker	overpaid	palliate
pachyderm	repaid	palliation
pacify	unpaid	palliative
pacific	pain	pallium
pacifically	painful	pallor
pacification	painless	palmetto
pacifier	painstaking	palmist
pacifism	paint	palmistry
pacifist	painted	palpate
pack	painter	palpability
package	pajama	palpable
packer	palace	palpation
packet	palatial	palpitate
pact	palanquin	palsy
pad	palate	palsied
paddle	palatable	paltry
paddock	paleography	pampas
padlock	paleontology	pamphlet
pagan	palette	panacea
page	palfrey	panchromatic
pagination	palimpsest	achromatic
pageant	palindrome	orthochromatic
pageantry	palisade	pancreas
	pall	pancreatic

pandemonium	paprika	paranoia
panegyric	par	paranoiac
panegyrical	parity	parapet
panegyrist	parable	paraphernalia
panegyrize	parabola	paraphrase
panel	parabolic	parasite
pang	parabolical	parasitic
panic	parachute	parcel
pannier	parade	parchment
panoply	paradigm	pardon
panorama	paradise	pardonable
panoramic	paradox	unpardonable
pansy	paradoxical	paregoric
pant	paraffin	parent
pantaloon	paragon	parentage
pantheon	paragraph	parental
panther	parallax	parenthesis
pantograph	parallel	parentheses
pantomime	parallelogram	parish
pantry	unparalleled	parishioner
papacy	paralyze	parliament
papal	paralysis	parliamentarian
paper	paralytic	parliamentary
newspaper	paralyzes	unparliamentary
papoose	paramount	parlor

parochial	participate	passion
parody	participant	dispassionate
parole	participle	impassioned
paroxysm	participial	passionate
paroxysmal	particle	passionless
parquet	particular	passive
parricide	particularity	impassive
parricidal	particularize	passivity
parrot	particularly	passover
parsley	partisan	passport
parsnip	partisanship	password
parsimony	partition	paste
parsimonious	partner	pasteboard
parson	partnership	pastel
parsonage	partridge	pastern
part	party	pastime
apart	paschal	pastor
apartment	pass	pastoral
compartment	impassable	pastorate
department	passable	pastry
partake	passage	pasture
parterre	passageway	pasturage
partial	passed	patch
partiality	past	patchwork
partially	passenger	patchy

patella	patrimonial	pay
patent	patriot	paid
patentable	patriotic	payable
patented	patriotism	payee
patentee	patrol	payees
paternal	patrolman	paymaster
paternalism	patron	payment
paternally	patronage	repaid
paternity	patroness	repay
path	patronize	unpaid
pathfinder	patronymic	peace
pathless	pattern	pacify
pathway	patterned	peaceable
pathology	paucity	peaceful
pathos	pauper	peacemaker
pathetic	pauperism	peacock
patient	pauperization	peanut
impatient	pauperize	pearl
patience	pause	peasant
patio	pave	peasantry
patriarch	pavement	pebble
patriarchal	pavilion	pebbly
patriarchate	pawn	pecan
patrician	pawnbroker	peccant
patrimony	pawnshop	peccadillo

peccancy

peccary

peck

pectoral

peculate

peculiar

peculiarity

peculiarly

pecuniary

pedagogue

pedagogic

pedagogical

pedagogy

pedal

pedant

pedantic

pedantical

pedantry

peddle

peddler

pedestal

pedestrian

pedestrianism

pediatrics

pedicular

pedigree

pediment

pedometer

peer

peerage

peeress

peerless

peevish

peg

Pegasus

pelican

pelisse

pellagra

pellet

pellucid

peltry

pelvis

pelvic

pemmican

pen

penholder

penknife

penance

penal

penalization

penalize

penalty

penology

penchant

pencil

pendant

pendulous

pendulum

penetrate

penetrability

penetrable

penetrant

penetration

penetrative

penguin

peninsula

peninsular

penitence

impenitent

penitent

penitential

penitentiary

penitently

pennant

penny

penniless	perceive	perfidy
pension	imperceptible	perfidious
pensionary	perceptible	perforate
pensioner	perception	perforates
pensive	perceptive	perforation
pent	perceptual	perforator
pentagon	percentage	perforce
pentameter	perchance	perform
Pentecost	percolate	performable
penthouse	percolation	performance
penult	percolator	performer
antepenult	percussion	perfume
penultimate	percussive	perfumer
penumbra	perdition	perfumery
penury	peregrination	perfunctory
penurious	peremptory	perfunctorily
peon	peremptorily	perfunctoriness
peony	peremptoriness	perhaps
people	perennial	peril
pepper	perfect	imperiled
peppermint	imperfect	perilous
pepsin	perfectible	perimeter
peradventure	perfection	period
perambulate	perfectly	periodic
percale	pluperfect	periodical

periodicity	permit	persecute
peripatetic	permissibility	persecution
periphery	permissible	persecutor
periphrastic	permission	persevere
periscope	permutation	perseverance
perish	pernicious	Persian
imperishable	peroration	persiflage
perishable	peroxide	persimmon
peristyle	perpendicular	persist
peritoneum	perpetrate	persistence
peritonitis	perpetrates	persistency
periwinkle	perpetration	persistent
perjure	perpetrator	person
perjured	perpetual	impersonal
perjurer	perpetually	impersonate
perjures	perpetuate	personable
perjury	perpetuated	personage
permanent	perpetuation	personal
permanence	perpetuator	personality
permanently	perpetuity	personalize
permanganate	perplex	personally
permeate	perplexed	personalty
permeability	perplexedly	personification
permeable	perplexity	personify
permeation	perquisite	personnel

perspective	perturb	pestilent
perspicacious	disturb	pestilential
perspicacity	perturbation	pet
perspicuity	perturbed	petal
perspicuous	peruse	petite
perspire	perusal	petition
perspiration	Peruvian	petitioner
perspires	pervade	petrel
persuade	pervasion	petrify
dissuade	pervasive	petrifaction
persuaded	perverse	petrifactive
persuader	perversely	petrol
persuades	perversion	petroleum
persuasion	perversity	petticoat
persuasive	perversive	petty
persuasiveness	pervert	pettily
suasion	perverted	pettiness
pert	pervious	pettish
pertain	impervious	petulant
pertained	pessimism	petulance
pertinacious	pessimist	petunia
pertinacity	pessimistic	pew
pertinence	pest	pewter
pertinency	pesthouse	phaëton
pertinent	pestilence	phalanx

phantom	phlegm	phrenology
phantasm	phlegmatic	phthisis
pharmacy	phlox	phylactery
pharmaceutic	phonic	physic
pharmaceutical	phonetic	physical
pheasant	phonetician	physician
phenol	phonetics	physicist
phenomenon	phonograph	physics
phenomena	phosphorus	physiognomy
phenomenal	phosphate	physiology
phial	phosphide	physique
philanderer	phosphoresce	piano
philanthropy	phosphorescence	pianist
philanthropic	phosphorescent	piazza
philanthropical	photo-electric	pica
philanthropist	photograph	picaresque
philatelic	photogravure	piccolo
philharmonic	photolithograph	pick
philology	photomicrograph	pickax
philosophy	photoplay	picker
philosopher	photostat	picket
philosophic	phrase	pickle
philosophical	phraseology	picnic
philosophize	phrenetic	picture
philter	frantic	pictograph

pictorial	pilot	piscatorial
pictorially	pimento	pistachio
picturesque	pimple	pistol
piety	pin	piston
pig	pinafore	pit
piggery	pincers	pitfall
piggish	pinch	pitted
pig-headed	pine	pitch
pigeon	pineapple	pitcher
pigment	ping-pong	pith
pigmentation	pink	pittance
pike	pinnace	pity
pikestaff	pinnacle	piteous
pilaster	pipe	pitiable
pilchard	pipage	pitied
pile	pipe clay	pitiful
piled	piped	pitiless
pilgrim	pipette	pitilessness
pilgrimage	piquant	pivot
pillage	piquancy	pivotal
pillar	pique	placard
pillion	pirate	placate
pillory	piracy	placability
pillow	piratic	placable
pillowcase	pirouette	place

placeman	plantation	plaudit
placement	planted	plausible
placer	planter	plausibility
placid	supplant	play
placidity	transplant	player
plagiarism	plantain	playful
plagiarist	plaster	playgoer
plagiarize	plastered	playground
plagiary	plasterer	playhouse
plague	plastic	playmate
plain	plasticity	plaything
plainer	plate	playtime
plainly	plateau	playwright
plainness	plated	please
plaint	plateful	displease
plaintiff	platen	pleasant
plaintive	plater	pleasantly
plan	platform	pleasantness
planned	platinum	pleasantry
planet	platinate	pleasurable
planetoid	platinic	pleasure
plangent	platitude	unpleasant
plank	platitudinize	plebeian
plant	platitudinous	plebiscite
implant	platoon	plectrum

pledge	plucky	pocket
pledgee	plug	pocketbook
pledger	plumb	pocketknife
pledgor	plumbed	poem
plenty	plumber	poet
plenarily	plumbic	poetaster
plenary	plumbago	poetic
plenipotentiary	plume	poetry
plenitude	plumage	poignant
plenteous	plump	poignancy
plentiful	plunder	poinciana
pleonasm	plunderer	poinsettia
plethora	plunge	point
plethoric	plunger	pointer
pleura	pluperfect	pointless
pleurisy	plural	points
pliant	plurality	poise
pliability	pluralize	poison
pliable	plus	poisoned
pliancy	plutocrat	poisoner
plight	plutocracy	poisonous
plow	plutocratic	poke
plowshare	pneumatic	poker
pluck	pneumatics	pole
pluckily	pneumonia	polar

polarity	polluted	pontiff
polarization	pollution	pontifical
polarize	polonaise	pontificate
polarizer	polonium	pontoon
polecat	poltroon	pony
polemic	polyandry	poor
polemical	polygamy	poorest
police	polyglot	poorhouse
policeman	polygon	poorly
policy	polygonal	poorness
policyholder	polyp	poplar
polish	pomade	poplin
polisher	pomegranate	popular
polite	pommel	depopulate
politely	pomology	populace
politeness	pompadour	popularity
politic	pompous	popularize
political	pomposity	popularly
politician	poncho	populate
politicly	pond	populous
politics	ponder	unpopular
polity	ponderable	porcelain
polka	ponderous	porch
pollen	pongee	porcupine
pollute	poniard	porphyry

porpoise	depose	post
porridge	expose	postage
porringer	impose	postal
port	poses	postcard
portable	propose	postdate
portage	suppose	posthaste
portal	position	postman
portcullis	deposition	postmark
porter	exposition	postmaster
porterhouse	imposition	poster
portfolio	preposition	posterior
porthole	proposition	posterity
portico	supposition	postern
portière	positive	postgraduate
portend	possess	posthumous
portent	dispossess	postilion
portentous	possession	postlude
portion	possessive	postpone
apportioned	possessor	postponement
portray	possessorship	postscript
portrait	possible	postulate
portraiture	impossible	postulant
portrayal	possibility	postulation
Portuguese	possibly	posture
pose	possum	pot

potter	pout	preamble
pottery	poverty	prearrange
potable	powder	prebendary
potation	powdery	precarious
potassium	power	precaution
potash	empower	precautionary
potato	powerful	precede
potent	powerless	precedence
impotent	practical	precedent
omnipotent	practicability	precedes
plenipotentiary	practicable	unprecedented
potency	practicality	precept
potentate	practically	preceptor
potential	practicalness	preceptress
potentiality	practice	precinct
potentially	practitioner	precious
potion	pragmatism	precipitate
pottage	pragmatic	precipice
pouch	pragmatist	precipitancy
poultice	prairie	precipitant
poultry	praise	precipitately
pounce	praised	precipitateness
pound	pray	precipitation
poundage	prayer	precipitous
poundcake	prayerful	precise

precision	predigestion	prelate
preclude	predilection	preliminary
preclusion	predispose	prelude
precocious	predisposition	premature
precocity	predominate	premeditate
preconceive	predominance	premeditation
preconception	predominant	premier
precursor	preeminent	premise
precursory	preempt	premium
predacious	preemption	premonition
depredation	preface	premonitory
predacity	prefatory	preoccupation
predatory	prefect	preoccupied
predecease	prefer	prepare
predecessor	preferability	preparedness
predestine	preferable	unprepared
predestination	preference	prepay
predetermine	preferential	prepaid
predicament	preferentially	prepayment
predicate	preferment	preponderate
predict	prefix	preponderance
predictable	prehistoric	preponderant
prediction	prejudge	preposition
unpredictable	prejudice	prepositional
predigest	prejudicial	prepossess

prepossession	presidency	pretext
preposterous	president	pretty
prerequisite	presidential	prettily
prerogative	press	prettiness
presage	pressman	pretzel
presbyterian	pressure	prevail
prescient	presswork	prevalence
nescient	prestige	prevalent
omniscient	prestidigitator	prevaricate
prescience	presume	prevarication
prescribe	presumable	prevaricator
prescription	presumedly	prevent
prescriptive	presumer	preventability
present	presumption	preventable
presence	presumptive	prevention
presentability	presumptuous	preventive
presentable	pretend	previous
presentation	pretended	prevision
presently	pretender	price
presentiment	pretense	priced
preserve	pretension	priceless
preservation	pretentious	prices
preservative	preterit	prickle
preserver	preternatural	prickly
preside	supernatural	pride

priest	printery	probate
priestess	prior	probation
priesthood	priority	probity
priestly	prism	problem
primal	prismatic	problematic
primary	prison	proceed
primarily	imprisoned	procedure
primate	prisoner	procession
primacy	pristine	processional
primeval	private	process
primitive	privacy	processes
primogeniture	privateer	proclaim
primordial	privately	proclamation
prince	privateness	proclivity
princeliness	privation	procrastinate
princely	deprive	procrastination
princess	privet	procrastinator
principal, principle	privilege	proctor
principality	privy	procure
principally	privily	procurable
unprincipled	privity	procuration
print	probable	procurement
printable	improbable	prodigal
printed	probability	prodigality
printer	probably	prodigy

prodigious	profile	prohibitive
produce	profit	prohibitory
by-product	profitable	project
produced	profitless	projectile
producer	profligate	projection
produces	profligacy	projector
product	profound	proletarian
production	profoundness	proletariat
productive	profundity	prolific
productivity	profuse	prolix
profane	profusely	prolixity
profanation	profuseness	prologue
profanity	profusion	prolong
profess	progeny	prolongate
professed	progenitor	prolongation
profession	prognosis	promenade
professional	prognostic	prominent
professionalism	prognosticate	prominence
professionally	program	promiscuous
professor	progress	promiscuity
professorial	progression	promiscuously
professorship	progressive	promiscuousness
proffer	prohibit	promise
proficient	prohibition	promised
proficiency	prohibitionist	promissory

promontory	propellant	proponent
promote	propeller	proprietor
promoted	propulsion	proprietary
promoter	propensity	propriety
promotion	proper	prorate
prompt	property	pro rata
prompted	prophet	prorogue
prompter	prophecy	prosaic
promptitude	prophesy	proscenium
promptly	prophetic	proscribe
promptness	prophylactic	proscription
promulgate	propinquity	proscriptive
promulgation	propitiate	prosecute
pronoun	propitiation	prosecution
pronounce	propitiatory	prosecutor
pronounceable	propitious	proselyte
pronounced	proportion	prosody
pronouncement	disproportionate	prospect
pronunciation	proportionable	prospective
proof	proportional	prospector
propagate	proportionate	prospectus
propaganda	propose	prosper
propagandist	proposal	prospered
propagation	proposition	prosperity
propel	propound	prosperous

prostrate

prostration

protagonist

protect

protection

protectionist

protective

protector

protectorate

unprotected

protégé

protein

protest

Protestant

Protestantism

protestation

protocol

protoplasm

prototype

protoxide

protract

protraction

protractive

protractor

protrude

protrusion

protrusive

protuberance

protuberant

proud

prouder

proudest

proudly

prove

provable

proved

proven

proverb

proverbial

provide

improvident

providence

provident

providential

provider

provision

provisional

province

provincial

provincialism

provinciality

provincially

proviso

provisory

provoke

provocation

provocative

provost

proximate

approximate

proximity

proximo

proxy

prudent

imprudently

prudence

prudential

prurient

Prussian

psalm

psalmist

psalmody

pseudonym

psychic

psychiatrist

psychiatry	pulmonary	pungency
psychical	pulmotor	punish
psychoanalysis	pulpit	punishable
psychology	pulse	punished
psychopathic	pulsate	punishment
ptomaine	pulsation	punitive
public	pulsator	puny
publication	pulsatory	pupil
publicist	pulverize	purblind
publicity	pulverization	purchase
publicly	pulverizer	purchaser
publish	pumice	pure
publisher	pump	impure
pucker	pumpkin	purely
pudding	punch	purification
puddle	punctilio	purifier
pueblo	punctilious	purify
pugilism	punctual	purism
pugilist	punctuality	purist
pugilistic	punctually	Puritan
pugnacity	unpunctual	purity
pugnacious	punctuate	purge
puissant	punctuation	purgatory
puissance	puncture	purlieu
pullet	pungent	purloin

purloined	pursued	putrefactive
purple	pursuit	putrescence
purplish	purulent	putrescent
purport	purvey	putrid
purported	purveyance	putty
purpose	purveyor	puzzle
purposeful	purview	pygmy
purposeless	pusillanimity	pyorrhea
purposely	pusillanimous	pyramid
purse	pustule	pyramidal
purser	put	pyre
pursue	putative	pyrography
pursuance	putrefy	pyrometer
pursuant	putrefaction	pyrotechnics

Q	quarry	unquestionable
quackery	quart	unquestioned
quadrangle	quarter	quibble
quadrant	quartered	quick
quadruped	quarterly	quicken
quadruple	quartermaster	quicklime
quadruplex	quartile	quickness
quadruplicate	quartz	quicksand
quagmire	quatrain	quicksilver
quail	quaver	quick-witted
quaint	quay	quiescent
quaker	quayage	quiet
qualify	queen	quieted
disqualify	queer	quietly
qualification	quench	quietness
qualified	quenchless	quietude
qualitative	unquenchable	quietus
quality	querulous	quill
unqualified	query	quilt
qualm	quest	quinine
quantity	question	quinquennial
quantitative	questionable	quintessence
quarantine	questioned	quintet
quarrel	questioner	quire
quarrelsome	questionnaire	quirk

quit

quitclaim

quitrent

quittance

quitter

quite

quiver

quixotic

quiz

quizzical

quoin

quoit

quondam

quorum

quota

quote

quotable

quotation

quoth

quotidian

quotient

R

rabbi

rabbit

rabble

rabid

rabies

raccoon

race

raced

racer

racial

racially

racily

raciness

racket

raconteur

radiate

radiance

radiancy

radiant

radiated

radiation

radiator

radical

eradicate

radicalism

radically

radio

radioactive

radiogram

radiophone

radiotelegraphy

radiotelephone

radish

radium

radius

radial

radially

radii

radiuses

raffle

raft

ragamuffin

raglan

ragout

raid

rail

railhead

raillery

railroad

railway

raiment

rain

rainbow

raindrop

rained

rainfall

rainier

rainiest

raisin

ramble

rambler

ramify

ramification

ramp

rampage

rampant

rampart

ranch

rancher

ranchero

ranchman

rancho

rancid

rancidly

rancor		rascality		rattle	
rancorous		rascally		rattler	
random		rash		rattlesnake	
rank		rasher		rattly	
rankle		rashest		raucous	
ransack		rashly		ravage	
ransom		rashness		ravel	
rapacity		raspberry		raven	
rapacious		rate		ravenous	
rapid		rated		ravine	
rapidity		rather		ravish	
rapidly		ratify		raw	
rapier		ratification		rawboned	
rapport		ratio		rawhide	
rapture		ratiocination		rawness	
rapturous		ration		ray	
rare		rational		rayless	
rarefaction		irrational		react	
rarefy		rationalism		reaction	
rarely		rationalist		reactionary	
rareness		rationalistic		reenact	
rarer		rationalization		read	
rarest		rationalize		readability	
rarity		rationally		readable	
rascal		rattan		reader	

readjust	reason	recapitulate
readjustment	reasonable	recapture
readmission	reasoned	recast
ready	unreasonable	recede
readily	reassemble	recession
readiness	reassert	receipt
reaffirm	reassume	receive
reagent	reassure	receivability
real	rebate	receivable
realism	rebel	receiver
realist	rebellion	receivership
realistic	rebellious	receives
reality	rebind	recent
realizable	rebirth	reception
realization	reborn	receptacle
realize	rebound	receptive
really	rebuff	receptivity
realty	rebuild	recipient
unreal	rebus	recess
reanimate	rebut	recession
reappear	rebuttal	recessional
reappearance	rebutter	recessive
reappoint	recalcitrant	recharge
reargue	recall	recharged
rearrange	recant	recipe

reciprocate	recognize	reconquer
reciprocal	recognition	reconsider
reciprocation	recognizable	reconstruct
reciprocative	recognizance	reconstruction
reciprocator	unrecognized	reconstructive
reciprocity	recoil	record
recite	recoiled	recorded
recital	recollect	recorder
recitation	recollection	recount
recitative	recommence	recounted
recited	recommend	recoup
reck	recommendation	recoupment
reckless	recommendatory	recourse
reckon	recommit	recover
reckoned	recommitted	irrecoverable
reckoner	reconcile	recoverable
reclaim	irreconcilable	recovery
irreclaimable	reconcilability	recreant
reclaimable	reconcilable	recreation
reclaimed	reconcilement	recriminate
reclamation	reconciliation	recrimination
recline	reconciliatory	recriminative
reclination	recondite	recriminatory
reclined	reconnaissance	recrudescence
recluse	reconnoiter	recruit

recruited	redness	reelect
recrystallize	redeem	reelection
rectangle	irredeemable	reembark
rectangular	redeemer	reenact
rectify	redemption	reenacted
rectification	redemptory	reenforce
rectifier	unredeemed	reenforcement
rectilinear	redirect	reengage
rectitude	redistribute	reengrave
rector	redolent	reenlist
rectory	redolence	reenlistment
recumbent	redouble	reenter · · · ·
recumbency	redoubt	reexamine
recuperate	redoubtable	reexamination
recuperation	redound	reexport
recuperative	reduce	refer
recuperatory	reduced	referable
recur	reducer	referee
recurrence	reduces	reference
recurrent	reducible	referendum
recusant	reduction	refine
red	redundant	refined
redden	redundance	refinement
reddened	redundancy	refiner
reddish	reecho	refinery

reflect	refrigerator	regatta
reflection	refuge	regenerate
reflective	refugee	regeneracy
reflector	refulgent	regeneration
reflex	refund	regenerative
reflexive	refunded	regenerator
reform	refurnish	unregenerate
reformation	refuse	regent
reformative	refusal	regicide
reformatory	refused	regimen
reformed	refuses	regiment
reformer	refute	regimental
refract	refutation	region
refraction	regain	regional
refractive	regained	register
refractivity	regal	registered
refractor	regally	registrar
refractory	regale	registration
refrain	regalia	registry
refrained	regard	regnant
refresh	disregard	regret
refreshment	regardful	regretful
refrigerate	regardless	regrettable
refrigeration	regards	regular
refrigerative	unregarded	irregular

regularity	rejoice	relentless
regulate	rejoiced	relevant
regulatory	rejoices	irrelevant
regurgitate	rejoin	relevance
regurgitation	rejoinder	relevancy
rehabilitate	rejuvenate	reliable
rehabilitation	rejuvenation	reliability
rehearse	rejuvenescence	reliance
rehearsal	rekindle	self-reliant
reimburse	relapse	unreliable
reimbursement	relate	relief
reimport	related	relievable
reimportation	relation	religion
reincarnation	relational	irreligious
reindeer	relationship	religious
reinstate	relative	relinquish
reinsure	relativity	relinquishment
reinvigorate	relax	relish
reissue	relaxation	reluctant
reiterate	relaxed	reluctance
reiteration	relaxes	remain
reject	release	remainder
dejected	relegate	remained
eject	relegation	remand
rejection	relent	remark

remarkable	remonstration	renunciatory
remarry	remonstrative	renovate
remedy	remorse	renovated
irremediable	remorseful	renovation
remediable	remorseless	renown
remedial	remote	renowned
remember	remoteness	rent
remembrance	remount	rental
remind	remove	rented
reminder	irremovable	reopen
remindful	removable	reorder
reminiscent	removal	reorganize
reminiscence	remunerate	repair
remiss	remuneration	irreparable
remission	remunerative	repaired
remit	renaissance	reparable
remittal	render	reparation
remittance	rendition	reparative
remittent	renegade	repartee
remitter	renew	repast
remnant	renewable	repatriate
remonstrate	renewal	repay
remonstrance	renominate	repaid
remonstrant	renounce	repayment
remonstrates	renunciation	repeal

repealed	replant	unrepresented
repeat	replanted	repress
repeatedly	replenish	irrepressible
repeater	replenishment	repression
repetition	replete	repressive
repel	repletion	reprieve
repelled	replevin	reprimand
repellence	replica	reprint
repellent	reply	reprisal
repulse	report	reproach
repent	reporter	irreproachable
repentance	repose	reproachful
repentant	reposeful	reprobate
repented	reposes	reprobation
repercussion	repository	reproduce
repercussive	repossess	reproduced
repertoire	reprehend	reproducer
repertory	reprehensibility	reproduces
repetition	reprehensible	reproduction
repetitious	reprehension	reproductive
repine	reprehensive	reprove
repined	represent	reproof
replace	misrepresent	reptile
replaced	representation	reptilian
replacement	representative	republic

republican	requital	residential
republicanism	reredos	residue
republish	resale	residual
repudiate	resold	residuary
repudiated	rescind	residuum
repudiation	rescript	resign
repugnant	rescue	resignation
repugnance	rescued	resigned
repulse	rescuer	resignedly
repulsed	research	resilient
repulsion	resemble	resilience
repulsive	resemblance	resiliency
repurchase	resent	resin
repute	resented	resist
disrepute	resentful	irresistible
reputable	resentment	resistance
reputation	reserve	resistant
request	reservation	resistibility
requiem	reserved	resistible
require	reservoir	resistivity
requirement	reship	resistless
requires	reside	resolve
requisite	residence	irresolute
requisition	residency	resoluble
requite	resident	resolute

resolution	respirator	restrained
resolvable	respiratory	restraint
resolved	respite	unrestrained
resolvent	resplendent	restrict
resonant	resplendence	restriction
resonance	resplendency	restrictive
resonator	respond	unrestricted
resort	respondent	result
resorted	response	resultant
resound	irresponsibility	results
resounded	irresponsible	resume
resource	responsible	resumable
resourceful	responsive	resumption
respect	rest	résumé
disrespect	rested	resurgent
irrespective	restful	resurgence
respectability	restless	resurrect
respectable	rests	resurrected
respecter	restate	resurrection
respectful-ly	restaurant	resuscitate
respective	restitution	resuscitation
respects	restore	retail
respire	restoration	retailed
respirable	restorative	retailer
respiration	restrain	retain

retained

retainer

retention

retentive

retentivity

retaliate

retaliation

retaliative

retaliatory

retard

retardation

retell

reticent

reticence

reticule

retina

retinal

retinue

retire

retired

retirement

retires

retort

retouch

retrace

retraceable

retract

retractile

retraction

retractive

retractor

retreat

retreated

retrench

retrenchment

retrial

retribution

retributive

retrieve

irretrievable

retrievable

retriever

retroactive

retrocession

retrograde

retrogression

retrogressive

retrospect

retrospection

retrospective

return

returnable

reunion

reunite

revalue

reveal

revelation

revelry

revenge

revenged

revengeful

revenue

reverberate

reverberant

reverberation

reverberative

reverberator

reverberatory

revere

irreverent

reverence

reverend

reverent

reverential

reverently

reverie	revivification	rhetorical
reverse	revivify	rhetorician
reversal	survive	rheumatism
reverses	revoke	rheumatic
reversible	irrevocable	rheumatoid
reversion	revocable	rhinestone
reversionary	revocation	rhinitis
revert	revolt	rhinoceros
revertible	revolve	rhubarb
revetment	revolution	rhythm
revictual	revolutionary	rhythmic
review	revolutionist	rhythmical
reviewed	revolutionize	ribald
reviewer	revolver	ribaldry
revile	revulsion	ribband
reviled	revulsive	ribbon
revilement	reward	rich
revise	rewarded	enrich
reviser	rewrite	richer
revision	rhapsody	riches
revisit	rhapsodic	richest
revitalize	rhapsodist	richly
vitalization	rhapsodize	richness
revive	rheostat	ride
revival	rhetoric	ridden

rider	ringer	ritually
riderless	ringleader	rival
ridicule	ringlet	rivalry
ridiculous	ringmaster	river
riffraff	riot	riverside
rifle	rioted	rivet
rifled	riotous	road
rifleman	riparian	roadbed
right	ripe	roadstead
right-angled	ripen	roadster
righteous	ripened	roadway
righteousness	ripeness	roam
rightful	riper	roamed
right-hand	ripest	roamer
rightly	ripple	roast
rightness	ripsaw	roaster
rigid	rise	robin
rigidity	arises	robust
rigidly	risen	rodent
rigor	risible	rodman
rigorous	risibility	rogue
ring	risk	roguery
ringbolt	rite	roguish
ringbone	ritual	roguishly
ringed	ritualistic	Roman

romance	rough	rubberize
romantic	roughcast	rubbery
romanticism	roughdry	rubbish
rondeau	roughen	rubicund
rookery	rougher	ruble
room	roughest	ruddy
roomer	roughhew	ruddily
roomful	roughly	ruddiness
roommate	roughness	rude
roomy	roulette	rudely
rosary	round	rudeness
rot	roundhouse	ruder
rotten	roundly	rudiment
rottenness	roundness	rudimental
rotate	roundsman	rudimentary
rotary	rout	rueful
rotation	route	ruffian
rotative	routed	ruffle
rotator	routine	ruffled
rotatory	royal	ruin
rotor	royalism	ruination
rotund	royally	ruined
rotunda	royalty	ruinous
rotundity	rub	rule
rouge	rubber	ruled

ruler	rumple	rushed
rumble	rumpus	russet
ruminate	runner	rust
ruminant	rupture	rustic
rumination	rural	rusticate
ruminative	ruralize	rusticity
rummage	rurally	ruthenium
rumor	rush	ruthless

S

Sabbath
sabbatical
sable
saccharin
sacerdotal
sachem
sachet
sacrament
sacramental
sacred
sacrifice
sacrificial
sacrilege
sacrilegious
sacristy
sacristan
sacrosanct
sad
sadden
sadness
safe
safe-conduct
safeguard
safe-keeping

safely
safeness
safety
unsafe
saffron
sagacity
sagacious
sahib
saint
sainted
saintliness
saintly
salad
salamander
salary
salaried
sale
resale
salability
salable
salesman
wholesale
salient
salience
saline

saliva
salivate
salivation
salmon
salon
saloon
salt
saltcellar
salted
saltpeter
salty
salubrious
salute
salutary
salutation
salutatorian
salutatory
salvage
salvation
salve
same
sameness
samovar
sample
example

exemplar	sapphire	satirize
sampler	saraband	satisfy
sanatory	sarcasm	dissatisfy
sanatorium	sarcastic	satisfaction
sanctify	sarcoma	satisfactory
sanctification	sarcophagus	unsatisfactory
sanctimonious	sarcophagi	saturate
sanction	sardine	saturation
sanctitude	sardonic	saturnine
sanctity	sardonyx	sauce
sanctuary	sarsaparilla	saucepan
sanctum	sartorial	saucer
sand	sassafras	saucily
sandal	satanic	sauciness
sane	satchel	saucy
insane	satiate	sauerkraut
sanity	insatiable	saunter
sanguine	satiable	sausage
consanguinity	satiation	savage
sanguinary	satiety	savagely
sanitary	satin	savagery
insanitary	satire	savanna
sanitation	satiric	save
sapient	satirical	savable
saponify	satirist	saved

savior	scapular	scherzo
savor	scarab	schism
saw	scarce	schismatic
sawdust	scarcity	schist
sawhorse	scarf	school
sawn	scarify	scholar
sawyer	scarification	scholarly
Saxon	scarlatina	scholarship
saxophone	scarlet	scholastic
scabbard	scatter	scholasticism
scaffold	scattered	schoolbook
scald	scavenger	schoolboy
scallop	scenario	schoolhouse
scalp	scene	schoolmaster
scalpel	scenery	schoolroom
scandal	scenic	schooner
scandalization	scenical	sciatica
scandalize	scent	science
scandalous	scented	scientific
Scandinavian	scepter	scientist
scansion	schedule	scimitar
scant	scheme	scintilla
scantily	schematic	scintillant
scantiness	schematize	scintillate
scapula	schemer	scintillation

scion	scrupulous	unseasonable
scissors	unscrupulous	secede
scoff	scrutiny	secession
scoffer	scrutinize	secessionist
scope	scuffle	seclude
scorch	scullion	secluded
score	sculptor	seclusion
scorn	sculptural	second
scorned	sculpture	secondarily
scornful	scum	secondary
scorpion	scurrility	seconded
Scotch	scurrilous	seconder
scoundrel	scurvy	secondly
scourge	scythe	secret
scraper	seal	secrecy
scrawl	sealed	secreted
screw	sealskin	secretion
scribble	search	secretive
script	research	secretly
scriptural	searcher	secretory
scripture	searchlight	secretary
scroll	season	secretarial
scrub	seasonable	secretariat
scruple	seasonal	sect
scrupulosity	seasoned	nonsectarian

sectarian	seducible	selection
sectary	seduction	selective
section	seductive	selectivity
sectional	sedulous	selectman
sectionalism	seemly	selector
sectionalize	unseemly	selenium
sectionally	seepage	self
sector	seersucker	self-assertion
secular	seethe	self-assured
secure	segment	self-command
securely	segmental	self-complacency
security	segmentary	self-conceit
sedan	segmentation	self-confidence
sedate	segregate	self-conscious
sedateness	segregation	self-contained
sedative	seismograph	self-contradiction
sedentary	seismology	self-contradictory
sediment	seize	self-control
sedimentary	seizable	self-deceit
sedimentation	seized	self-defense
sedition	seizes	self-denial
seditious	seizure	self-destruction
seduce	seldom	self-determined
seducer	select	self-educated
seduces	selected	self-esteem

self-evident	self-sufficient	senatorially
self-examination	self-supporting	senatorship
self-executing	self-surrender	send
self-government	selvage	godsend
self-importance	semantics	missent
self-induced	semaphore	sender
self-indulgence	semblance	sent
self-interest	semester	senile
selfish	semiannual	senility
selfishness	semicircle	senior
unselfish	semicircular	seniority
self-love	semicivilized	sensate
self-made	semicolon	insensate
self-perception	semidetached	sensation
self-possessed	semifinal	sensational
self-reliance	seminar	sensationalism
self-renunciation	seminary	sensationally
self-reproach	semiofficial	sense
self-respect	semiopaque	senseless
self-restraint	semiprecious	sensibility
self-righteous	semitransparent	sensible
self-sacrifice	semiweekly	sensitive
self-satisfied	senate	sensitivity
self-starter	senator	sensitization
self-styled	senatorial	sensitize

sensitizer	separation	serenata
sensory	separatist	serene
sensual	separative	serenely
sensualism	separator	sereneness
sensuality	sepia	serenity
sensually	sepoy	serf
sensuous	sepsis	serge
sentence	septic	sergeant
sententious	antiseptic	serial
sentient	sepulcher	serially
sentience	sepulchral	series
sentiency	sepulture	serious
sentiment	sequel	seriousness
sentimental	sequence	sermon
sentimentalism	sequester	sermonize
sentimentalist	sequestered	serpent
sentimentality	sequestrate	serpentine
sentimentalize	sequestration	serum
sentimentally	sequin	serous
sentinel	Sequoia	serve
sentry	seraph	servant
separate	seraphic	served
separability	seraphim	server
separable	Serbian	service
separately	serenade	serviceable

servile	sextant	shamble
servility	sextet	shame
servitor	sexton	shamefaced
servitude	shabby	shameful
sesame	shabbily	shameless
session	shabbiness	shampoo
settee	shackle	shamrock
settle	shade	shanghai
settled	shadier	shank
settlement	shadiest	shan't
settler	shadily	shape
unsettled	shadiness	shaped
sever	shadow	shapeless
severable	shadowy	shapeliness
severance	shady	shapely
several	shaft	shaper
severalty	shake	share
severe	shaker	shared
severity	shakily	shareholder
sew	shakiness	sharer
sewed	Shakespearean	shark
sewn	shall	sharp
sewer	shallow	sharpen
sewage	shallowly	sharpened
sewerage	shallowness	sharpener

sharper	sherbet	shiver
sharpest	sheriff	shock
sharpness	sherry	shoddy
sharpshooter	shiftless	shoe
sharp-witted	shilling	shoes
shatter	shimmer	shoot
non-shatterable	shimmery	shot
shattered	shingle	shop
shear	ship	shopkeeper
sheared	reship	shoplifter
shears	shipboard	shopper
sheath	shipbuilder	shopworn
sheepish	shipload	workshop
sheer	shipmate	short
sheerer	shipment	shortage
sheerest	shipowner	shortcake
sheerly	shipper	shortcoming
sheerness	shipshape	shorten
shelf	shipwreck	shorter
shelves	shipwright	shortest
shellac	shipyard	shorthand
shellfish	unship	short-lived
shelter	shire	shortly
sheltered	shirk	shortness
shelterless	shirt	shortsighted

shortstop		shunt		sidewalk	
should		shut		sight	
shoulder		shutdown		sightless	
shovel		shutter		sightliness	
shower		shy		sightly	
showy		shied		sight-seeing	
showily		shier		unsightly	
showiness		shiest		signal	
shrewd		shyly		signaler	
shrift		shyness		signalize	
shrine		sibilant		signally	
shrink		sibyl		signature	
shrank		sick		signatory	
shrinkage		sickened		unsigned	
shrive		sickliness		signify	
shriven		sickly		insignificant	
shroud		sickness		significant	
shrub		side		significantly	
shrug		beside		signification	
shudder		sideboard		silence	
shuddered		sidelong		silencer	
shuffle		sidepiece		silent	
shuffled		sides		silhouette	
shun		sidestep		silicon	
shunned		sidetrack		silica	

silicate		since		sirloin	
silk		sincere		sirup	
silken		insincere		sister	
silkiness		sincerely		sisterhood	
silkworm		sincerity		sister-in-law	
silt		sinecure		sisterly	
silver		sinew		situation	
silversmith		sinewy		situated	
silverware		singer		size	
silvery		single		sizable	
simian		singleness		sizes	
similar		singly		skeleton	
similarity		singular		skeletonize	
simile		singularity		skeptic	
similitude		singularly		skeptical	
simple		sinister		skepticism	
simpler		sinner		sketch	
simplest		sinuous		sketchily	
simplicity		sinuosity		skewer	
simplification		sinus		skill	
simplify		siphon		skilled	
simply		siphoned		skillful	
simulate		sir		unskillful	
dissimulation		sire		skirmish	
simultaneous		siren		skirt	

sky	sleep	slipshod
skies	sleeper	sloop
skylark	sleepily	sloth
skylight	sleepiness	slothful
skyrocket	sleepless	slouch
skyscraper	slept	slough
skyward	slender	slovenly
slack	slenderer	slow
slacken	slenderest	slower
slackness	slenderness	slowest
slander	slice	slowly
slanderer	slight	slowness
slanderous	slighter	sludge
slant	slightest	sluggard
slanted	slightly	sluggish
slatternly	slightness	sluice
slaughter	sliminess	sluiceway
slaughtered	slimily	slumber
slaughterer	slimness	slumberer
slaughterhouse	sling	slumberous
slave	slip	slung
enslavement	slipknot	underslung
slaveholder	slippage	slur
slavery	slipper	slush
slavish	slipperiness	sly

slier	smoothed	snuffle
sliest	smoothen	soak
slyly	smoother	soap
small	smoothest	soapiness
smaller	smoothness	sober
smallest	smother	social
smallness	smothered	sociability
smallpox	smudge	sociable
smart	smuggle	socialism
smarten	smuggled	socialist
smarter	snapshot	socialistic
smartest	snarl	socialization
smartly	sneer	socialize
smartness	snort	socially
smelt	snout	society
smile	snow	sociology
smiles	snowball	sodden
smite	snowfall	sodium
smoke	snowflake	soda
smokeless	snowplow	sofa
smoker	snowshoe	soft
smokestack	snowslide	soften
smokiest	snowstorm	softness
smolder	snowy	soil
smooth	snuff	sojourn

sojourned	solidity	somewhere
sojourner	solidly	somnambulism
solace	solidness	somnambulist
solar	soliloquy	somnolent
solder	soliloquize	sonata
soldier	solitaire	song
soldierly	solitary	songster
soldiery	solitude	son-in-law
solecism	solstice	sonnet
solemn	solution	sonorous
solemnity	solubility	sonority
solemnization	soluble	soon
solemnize	solve	sooner
solemnly	solvable	soonest
solenoid	solvent	soothe
solicit	solvency	soothed
solicitation	somber	sophisticate
solicitor	some	sophistication
solicitous	somebody	sophistry
solicitude	somehow	sophomore
unsolicited	someone	soporific
solid	something	soprano
solidarity	sometime	sorcery
solidification	sometimes	sorcerer
solidify	somewhat	sordid

sordidness	southeast	spasmodically
sorority	southeasterly	speak
sorrow	southeastern	bespeak
sorrowful	southerly	speaker
sorry	southerner	spoke
sort	southernmost	spoken
assorted	southwest	unspeakable
sorted	southwesterly	special
sought	souvenir	especial
unsought	sovereign	specialist
soul	sovereignty	specialization
soulful	space	specialize
soulless	spacious	specially
sound	spandrel	specialty
sounded	spangle	specific
soundest	spaniel	specification
soundless	Spanish	specify
soundly	spare	unspecified
soundness	spared	specie
unsound	spark	species
soup	sparkle	specimen
source	sparse	specious
resourceful	sparsity	spectacle
sources	spasm	spectacular
south	spasmodic	spectacularly

spectator	sphinx	spiritualize
specter	spice	spiritually
spectral	spiciness	spirituous
spectroscope	spider	spite
spectrum	spidery	despite
speculate	spigot	spiteful
speculum	spike	splendor
speech	spill	splendid
speechless	spilled	splendorous
speechmaker	spillway	splint
speed	spin	splinter
speedily	spinster	spoil
speedometer	spun	spoilage
speedway	spinach	spoiled
spell	spine	spoliate
misspell	spinal	spoliation
speller	spineless	spoliative
spend	spinet	spoliator
misspent	spiral	sponge
spendthrift	spire	sponsor
spermaceti	spirit	spontaneity
sphere	spiritless	spontaneous
hemisphere	spiritualism	spoon
spherical	spiritualist	spoonful
spheroid	spirituality	tablespoon

teaspoon	squad	stability
sport	squadron	stabilization
sportive	squall	stabilize
sportsman	squalor	stabilizer
sportsmanship	squalid	stable
spot	squalidity	staccato
spotless	squander	stadium
spotlight	square	stadia
spotted	squash	stadiums
spouse	squat	staff
sprawl	squatter	staves
sprightly	squaw	stage
spring	squeak	stagecoach
sprinkle	squeal	stagecraft
sprinkled	squeamish	stagger
sprinkler	squeegee	stagnate
sprocket	squeeze	stagnant
sprout	squeezed	stagnation
spunk	squib	stain
spur	squid	stained
spurious	squint	stair
spurn	squirm	staircase
spurt	squirrel	stairway
spy	squirt	stalactite
spied	stabile	stalagmite

stalk	stapler	stately
stallion	star	statement
stalwart	starfish	stateroom
stamina	starlight	statesman
stammer	starry	static
stammerer	starch	hydrostatics
stamp	stare	station
stampede	stared	stationary
stanch	stark	stationer
stanchion	starling	stationery
stand	start	statistics
notwithstanding	started	statistical
stand-off	startle	statistically
standpipe	startled	statistician
standpoint	starve	statue
standstill	starvation	statuary
stood	starved	statuesque
understood	state	statuette
withstand	estate	stature
withstood	instate	status
standard	misstatement	statute
standardization	reinstate	statutory
standardize	statehood	stay
stanza	statehouse	stayed
staple	stateliness	stead

instead	stein	sternly
steadfast	stellar	sternness
steady	stem	sternum
steadily	stemmed	stertorous
steadiness	stencil	stethoscope
unsteady	stenography	stevedore
steal	stenographer	stew
stolen	step	steward
stealth	stepchild	stick
stealthier	stepdaughter	sticker
stealthily	stepladder	stickful
steam	stepmother	stickier
steamboat	stepson	stickiest
steamed	stereopticon	stickiness
steamer	stereoscope	sticky
steamship	stereotype	stiff
steamy	sterilize	stiffen
steel	sterile	stiffer
steep	sterility	stiffest
steeper	sterilization	stiffness
steepest	sterilizer	stifle
steeple	sterling	stigma
steer	stern	stigmas
steerage	sterner	stigmata
steersman	sternest	stigmatic

stigmatism	stirrup	stone
stigmatize	stitch	stoned
stile	stock	stoneware
stiletto	stockade	stonework
still	stockbroker	stonily
distill	stockholder	stoniness
stillness	stockily	stony
stilly	stockiness	stood
stilt	stockings	stool
stilted	stockman	stoop
stimulate	stock-still	stop
stimulant	stocky	stoppage
stimulus	stockyard	stopped
sting	stogy	stopper
stinger	stoic	store
stung	stoical	storage
stint	stoicism	storehouse
stinted	stoke	storeroom
stipend	stokehold	stork
stipendiary	stoker	storm
stipple	stole	stormed
stippled	stolid	stormier
stipulate	stolidity	stormiest
stir	stolidly	stormily
stirred	stomach	storminess

stormy	strait-laced	strawberry
stout	strange	strawboard
stouter	estranged	streak
stoutest	strangely	streakily
stoutly	strangeness	streakiness
stoutness	stranger	streaky
stow	strangest	stream
stowage	strangle	streamed
stowaway	strangled	streamer
stowed	strangler	streamlet
straddle	strangles	streamline
straggle	strangulate	street
straggled	stratagem	strength
straggler	strategic	strengthen
straight	strategical	strengthened
straightedge	strategist	strenuous
straighten	strategy	stretch
straightened	stratify	stretcher
straightener	strata	strew
straightforward	stratification	strewn
straightway	stratum	striate
strait	stratums	striated
straiten	stratus	striation
straitened	substratum	strict
strait-jacket	straw	stricter

strictest	stroller	student
strictly	strong	studied
strictness	strength	studio
stricture	stronger	studious
stride	strongest	stuff
strident	stronghold	stuffier
strife	strongly	stuffiest
strike	strong-minded	stuffiness
striker	strontium	stuffy
stroke	structure	stultify
struck	structural	stultification
string	structurally	stumble
stringed	struggle	stump
stringier	struggler	stun
stringiest	strum	stunned
stringy	strummed	stunner
strung	strut	stunt
stringent	strutted	stunted
stringency	stub	stupefy
stripe	stubble	stupefacient
strive	stubborn	stupefaction
striven	stubbornness	stupor
strove	stucco	stupendous
stroll	stud	stupid
strolled	study	stupidity

stupidly	sub-basement	sublet
sturdy	subcellar	sublimate
sturdily	subcommittee	sublimated
sturdiness	subconscious	sublimation
sturgeon	subcontractor	sublime
stutter	subcutaneous	sublimer
style	subdeacon	sublimest
styled	subdivide	sublimity
stylish	subdivision	submarine
stylishness	subdue	submerge
stylist	subdued	submerged
stylistic	subeditor	submergence
stylographic	subequatorial	submerse
stylus	subgroup	submersible
styptic	subhead	submersion
Styx	subject	submit
suasion	subjection	submission
suave	subjective	submissive
suavely	subjectivity	submitted
suavity	subjoin	subnormal
subacid	subjugate	subofficer
subagent	subjugation	suborder
subaltern	subjugator	subordinate
subaqueous	subjunctive	coordinate
subarctic	sublease	subordination

subordinative	substantiation	subvert
suborn	substantive	subversion
subornation	substitute	subversive
suborner	substitution	subway
subpœna	substratum	succeed
subscribe	substrata	succeeded
subscriber	subtend	success
subscription	subterfuge	successful
subsequent	subterranean	succession
subserve	subtitle	successive
subservience	subtle	successor
subservient	subtile	unsuccessful
subside	subtler	succinct
subsidence	subtlest	succor
subsidy	subtlety	succotash
subsidiary	subtly	succulent
subsidize	subtract	succulence
subsist	subtraction	succumb
subsistence	subtrahend	such
subsists	subtreasury	suction
subsoil	subtropical	sudden
substance	suburb	suddenly
substantial	suburban	suddenness
substantially	suburbanite	sudorific
substantiate	subvention	sue

suable	sugary	sultry
sued	suggest	sum
sues	suggestibility	summation
suede	suggestible	summed
suet	suggestion	sumac
suffer	suggestive	summary
sufferable	suicide	summarily
sufferance	suicidal	summariness
sufferer	suit	summarization
suffice	suitability	summarize
insufficient	suitable	summer
sufficiency	suited	summerhouse
sufficient	suite	summery
suffix	sulk	summit
suffocate	sulkily	summon
suffocation	sulkiness	sumptuous
suffocative	sullen	sumptuary
suffragan	sullenness	sun
suffrage	sulphur	sunbeam
suffragette	sulphate	sunburn
suffragist	sulphide	sunburst
suffuse	sulphite	sundial
suffusion	sulphuric	sunless
sugar	sulphurous	sunlight
sugarplum	sultan	sunned

sunniness	superficially	supervene
sunrise	superfluous	supervention
sunset	superfluity	supervise
sunshine	superhuman	supervision
sunstroke	superimpose	supervisor
Sunday	superinduce	supervisory
sunder	superintend	supine
asunder	superintendence	supineness
sundry	superintendent	supper
sunk	superior	supplant
sunken	superiority	supplanted
superable	superlative	supple
insuperable	supernal	supplement
superabundant	supernatural	supplemental
superannuate	preternatural	supplementary
superannuation	supernaturalism	supplicate
superb	supernaturally	suppliant
supercalender	supernumerary	supplicant
supercargo	supersaturate	supplication
supercilious	superscribe	supplicatory
superdreadnaught	superscription	supply
supereminent	supersede	supplied
supererogation	supersensitive	support
superficial	superstition	supportable
superficiality	superstitious	supported

supporter	surf	surround
suppose	surface	surroundings
supposable	surfeit	survey
supposedly	surge	surveillance
supposition	surgeon	surveyor
supposititious	surgery	survive
suppress	surgical	revive
suppression	surly	survival
suppressive	surlier	survivorship
suppurate	surliest	susceptible
suppuration	surmise	susceptibility
suppurative	surmised	suspect
supreme	surmount	suspicion
supremacy	surmountable	suspicious
surbase	surmounted	unsuspected
surcease	surname	suspend
surcharge	surpass	suspended
surcingle	surplice	suspender
sure	surplus	suspense
surely	surplusage	suspension
sureness	surprise	sustain
surer	surprised	sustainable
surest	surrender	sustained
surety	surreptitious	sustenance
suretyship	surrogate	suture

suzerain	sweeten	swirl
suzerainty	sweetheart	Swiss
swagger	sweetish	switch
swain	sweetmeat	swivel
swallow	sweetness	swollen
swamp	swell	swoon
swan	swelled	swoop
swarm	swelter	sword
swarthy	swerve	swordfish
swarthier	swift	swordsman
swarthiest	swifter	sycamore
swastika	swiftest	sycophant
swath	swiftly	sycophancy
swathe	swiftness	sycophantic
sway	swill	syllable
swear	swim	syllabi
sweat	swam	syllabic
sweatily	swum	syllabicate
sweatiness	swindle	syllabication
sweatshop	swindler	syllabification
Swedish	swine	syllabify
sweep	swineherd	syllabus
sweet	swing	syllabuses
sweetbread	swung	syllogism
sweetbrier	swipe	syllogistic

symbol	symptom	synonym
symbolic	symptomatic	synonymous
symbolical	symptomatology	synopsis
symbolism	synagogue	synoptic
symbolist	synchronize	syntax
symbolization	synchronism	synthesis
symbolize	synchronous	synthesist
symmetry	syncopate	synthesize
symmetric	syncopation	synthetic
symmetrical	syncope	synthetical
sympathize	syndic	syringe
sympathetic	syndicalism	syrup
sympathizer	syndicate	system
sympathy	synecdoche	systematic
symphony	synod	systematical
symphonic	synodic	systematize
symposium	synodical	systemic

T

tabard
tabasco
tabernacle
table
  tableau
  tablecloth
  tablespoon
  tablet
  tableware
  tabloid
taboo
taboret
tabulate
  tabular
  tabularize
tachometer
tacit
  taciturn
  taciturnity
tackle
tact
  tactful
  tactile
  tactility

tactless
tactics
  tactical
  tactician
taffeta
tailor
taint
  tainted
take
  overtake
  takedown
  taken
  take-off
  took
  undertake
talent
  talented
talisman
talk
  talkative
  talker
tall
  taller
  tallest
  tallness

tamarack
tamarind
tambourine
tame
  tamely
  tamer
  tamest
  untamed
tamper
tanager
tandem
tang
tangent
  tangential
  tangerine
tangible
  intangible
  tangibility
tangle
  disentangle
  entangle
tank
  tankage
  tankard
  tanker

tanner		tart		tautology	
tannery		tartan		tavern	
tannic		tartar		tawdry	
tantalize		tartaric		tawny	
tantalization		task		tax	
tantalum		tassel		taxable	
tantamount		tasseled		taxation	
taper		taste		taxed	
tapestry		tasted		taxes	
tapioca		tasteful		taxi	
tapir		tasteless		taxicab	
tappet		taster		taximeter	
tarantula		tastily		taxidermy	
tarantella		tastiness		taxidermist	
tardy		tasty		teach	
tardier		tatter		taught	
tardiest		tattered		teachability	
tardily		tatters		teachable	
target		tattle		teacher	
tariff		tattoo		team	
tarlatan		tattooed		teamster	
tarnish		taunt		teamwork	
untarnished		taunted		tear	
tarpaulin		taut		tearful	
tarpon		tautness		tearless	

tears	telephone	tempestuous
tear	telephonic	template
tore	telephonically	temple
torn	telephony	templed
tease	telescope	tempo
teased	telescopic	temporal
teaspoon	telescopical	temporality
teaspoonful	tell	temporary
technic	telltale	temporarily
technical	told	temporization
technicality	tellurium	temporize
technician	temblor	temporizer
technique	temerity	tempt
technology	temerarious	temptation
tedium	temper	tempted
tedious	temperament	tempter
telautograph	temperamental	temptress
telegraph	temperamentally	tenable
telegram	temperance	untenable
telegrapher	intemperance	tenacity
telegraphic	temperate	pertinacious
telegraphical	temperately	pertinacity
telegraphy	temperateness	tenacious
telepathy	temperature	tenant
telepathic	tempest	tenancy

tenantable	tenser	terra cotta
tenanted	tensest	terrain
tenantless	tensile	terrapin
tenantry	tension	terrestrial
untenanted	tensional	terrify
tend	tensity	terrible
tended	tent	terrific
tendency	tentacle	terrifically
tender	tentative	territory
tendered	tenuity	territorial
tenderer	attenuated	territoriality
tenderest	tenuous	territorialize
tenderfoot	tepee	territorially
tenderloin	tepid	terror
tenderly	tercentenary	terrorism
tenderness	term	terrorist
tendon	termed	terroristic
tendril	terminable	terrorization
tenebrous	terminal	terrorize
tenement	terminally	terrorizer
tenet	terminate	terse
tennis	termination	terseness
tenon	terminology	terser
tenor	terminus	tersest
tense	terrace	tertiary

tessellate	texture	thenceforth
tessellation	than	thenceforward
test	thane	theocracy
tested	thank	theodolite
tester	thanked	theology
tests	thankful	theologian
untested	thankless	theory
testament	thanks	theorem
testamentary	thanksgiving	theoretic
testate	that	theorist
testator	thatch	theorize
testify	thaw	theorizer
testimonial	theater	theosophy
testimony	theatric	theosophic
tetanus	theatrical	theosophical
tether	theatricals	theosophist
tetragon	thee	therapy
tetragonal	theirs	therapeutic
tetralogy	theism	therapeutical
Teutonic	atheism	there
text	pantheism	thereabout
textbook	them	thereafter
textual	themselves	thereat
textually	then	thereby
textile	thence	therefore

therefrom	thickener	thinks
therein	thicker	unthinkable
thereinto	thicket	thirst
thereof	thickly	thirstily
thereon	thickness	thirstiness
thereto	thief	thirsty
theretofore	theft	this
thereupon	thievery	thistle
therewith	thievish	thither
therm	thigh	thole
thermal	thimble	thong
thermion	thin	thoracic
thermite	thinner	thorium
thermometer	thinness	thorn
thermometric	thinnest	thorough
thermometrical	thing	thoroughbred
thermostat	anything	thoroughfare
thesaurus	everything	thoroughly
these	nothing	thoroughness
thesis	plaything	those
theses	something	thou
thew	things	though
they	think	thought
thick	thinkable	thoughtful
thicken	thinker	thoughtless

thousand	thrived	thus
thousandfold	throve	thwart
thousands	throat	thy
thousandth	throatiness	thine
thrall	throb	thyself
thrash	throne	thyme
thread	dethrone	thyroid
threadbare	enthroned	tiara
threadworm	throng	Tibetan
threat	throttle	tide
threaten	through	tidewater
threatened	throughout	tidy
three	throw	tidier
threnody	threw	tidiest
threshold	thrown	tidiness
threw	thrush	untidy
thrice	thrust	tiger
thrift	thud	tight
spendthrift	thug	air-tight
thriftily	thumb	tighten
thriftiness	thump	tightened
thriftless	thunder	tighter
thrifty	thunderbolt	tightest
thrill	thunderous	tiled
thrive	thundershower	till

until	tinsel	toasted
tilt	tint	toastmaster
tilted	tinted	tobacco
timber	tiny	toboggan
time	tinier	toccata
time-honored	tiniest	tocsin
timekeeper	tirade	today
timeless	tire	toga
timely	tired	together
timepiece	tireless	toil
timer	tiresome	toilful
time-table	tissue	toilsome
timid	titanium	token
intimidate	tithe	told
timidity	titillate	untold
timidly	titivate	tolerate
timorous	title	tolerable
tin	title-page	tolerance
tinware	titular	tolerant
tincture	titmouse	toleration
tinder	titrate	tomahawk
tinge	titration	tomato
tingle	toad	tomb
tinker	toadstool	tombstone
tinkle	toast	tomorrow

ton	topography	totalizer
tonnage	torch	totally
tone	torment	totem
monotone	tormented	totter
tonal	tormentor	touch
tonality	tornado	touchable
tongue	torpedo	touchdown
tonight	torpor	touchily
tonsil	torpid	touchiness
tonsillitis	torque	touchstone
tonsure	torrent	untouched
tonsorial	torrential	tough
tontine	torrentially	toughen
tool	torrid	toughened
tooth	torridity	tougher
teeth	torsion	tour
toothache	torso	tourist
toothed	tort	tourmaline
toothless	tortoise	tournament
toothpick	tortuous	tourniquet
toothsome	tortuosity	tousle
top	torture	toward
topaz	total	towel
topic	totality	tower
topical	totalization	town

township	tradesman	tranquilization
toxic	tradition	tranquilize
toxicity	traditional	tranquillity
toxicology	traditionally	tranquilly
trace	traduce	transact
retrace	traffic	transaction
traceable	tragedy	transatlantic
traced	tragedian	transcend
tracer	tragic	transcendence
tracery	tragical	transcendent
trachea	train	transcendental
trachoma	trained	transcribe
track	trainer	transcript
trackage	trainman	transcription
trackless	traitor	transept
trackman	traitorous	transfer
tract	traitress	transferable
tractable	trajectory	transference
traction	trammel	untransferable
tractive	trammeled	transfigure
tractor	tramp	transfiguration
trade	trample	transfix
traded	tramway	transform
trade-mark	trance	transformation
trader	tranquil	transformer

transfuse	transmission	transubstantiation
transfusion	transmittal	transverse
transgress	transmitter	transversal
transgression	transmogrify	trapeze
transgressor	transmute	trauma
transient	transmutability	traumatic
transience	transmutable	travail
transit	transmutation	travel
transition	transom	traveler
transitional	transparency	traverse
transitionally	transparent	travesty
transitive	transpire	treachery
transitory	transpiration	treacherous
translate	transplant	treacle
translatable	transplantation	tread
translation	transplanted	trod
translator	transport	trodden
untranslatable	transportable	treadle
transliterate	transportation	treason
obliterate	transported	treasonable
translucence	transpose	treasure
translucent	transposes	treasured
transmit	transposition	treasurer
transmissibility	transship	treasures
transmissible	transubstantiate	treasury

treat	triangulate	trillium
treatise	tribe	trilogy
treatment	tribal	trim
treaty	tribesman	trimly
treble	tribulation	trimmed
tremble	tribune	trimmer
tremendous	tribunal	trimness
tremolo	tribute	trinity
tremor	tributary	trinket
tremulous	trick	trio
trench	trickery	triphthong
trenchancy	trickily	triple
trenchant	trickiness	triplet
trencher	trickster	triplex
trepan	trickle	triplicate
trephine	trickled	triplication
trepidation	tricycle	triply
intrepid	trident	triptych
trespass	triennial	trisect
trespasser	trifle	trite
trestle	trifler	triturate
triad	trigger	trituration
trial	trigonometry	triumph
triangle	trigonometric	triumphal
triangular	trillion	triumphant

triumvirate	truckman	trustful
triune	truckle	untrustworthy
trivial	truculent	truth
triviality	truculence	truthful
trivially	trudge	untruthful
troche	true	try
trolley	trueness	trial
trombone	truer	untried
troop	truest	tryst
trooper	truism	tsar
tropic	truly	tub
tropical	truth	tuba
troth	untrue	tube
troubadour	trumpet	tubular
trouble	trumpeter	tuber
troublesome	truncate	tubercle
troublous	truncheon	tubercular
trousers	trundle	tuberculin
trousseau	trunk	tuberculosis
trout	trust	tuberculous
trowel	distrust	tuberose
truant	entrust	tuition
truancy	mistrust	intuition
truck	trustee	tumble
truckage	trusteeship	tumor

tumult	turncoat	two-ply
tumultuous	turned	twosome
tune	turnout	two-step
tuned	turnpike	type
tuneful	turnip	typesetter
tuneless	turpentine	typewriter
tuner	turpitude	typewritten
tungsten	turquoise	typist
tunic	turret	typographer
tunnel	turtle	typography
turban	tutelage	typothetae
turbid	tutor	typhus
turbidity	twaddle	typhoid
turbidly	tweezers	typify
turbulent	twilight	typical
turbulence	twin	typification
tureen	twine	tyrant
turgid	twinkle	tyrannical
turgidity	twirl	tyrannicide
turkey	twist	tyrannize
turmeric	two	tyrannous
turmoil	two-faced	tyranny
turn	twofold	tyro
turnbuckle	two-handed	tzar

U

ubiquity	unable	unassailable
ubiquitous	inability	unassisted
ugly	unabridged	unassuming
ugliness	unaccented	unattached
ukase	unacceptable	unattainable
ukulele	unaccompanied	unattained
ulcer	unaccountable	unattempted
ulcerate	unaccustomed	unattended
ulceration	unadjusted	unauthenticated
ulcerative	unadorned	unauthorized
ulcerous	unadulterated	unavailable
ulna	unaffected	unavoidable
ulnar	unaided	unaware
ulster	unalloyed	unbalanced
ulterior	unalterable	unbecoming
ultimate	un-American	unbelief
ultimatum	unamiable	unbelievable
ultimo	unanimity	unbend
ultramarine	unanimous	unbidden
ultra-violet	unanswerable	unblemished
umbrage	unappeasable	unblushing
umbrella	unapproachable	unbound
umlaut	unappropriated	unbreakable
umpire	unarmed	unbusinesslike
	unasked	uncanny

unceremonious	unconstitutional	undercurrent
uncertain	uncontradicted	underestimate
uncertainty	uncontrollable	underexpose
unchallenged	uncontrolled	undergarment
unchangeable	unconventional	undergo
uncharitable	uncouth	undergraduate
uncial	uncover	underground
uncivilized	unction	undergrowth
unclaimed	unctuous	underhanded
unclassified	uncultivated	underline
uncle	undamaged	undermine
unclean	undaunted	undermined
uncleaned	undeceive	underneath
uncollectible	undecided	underproduction
uncomfortable	undecipherable	underrate
uncommon	undefended	underscore
uncommunicative	undefiled	undersell
uncomplimentary	undeliverable	undersized
uncompromising	undemocratic	underslung
unconcerned	undemonstrative	understand
unconditional	undeniable	misunderstand
unconquerable	under	misunderstood
unconscionable	underbid	understudy
unconscious	underbrush	undertake
unconsidered	undercharge	undertaker

undertook	undulant	unethical
undervalue	unduly	uneven
underwrite	undutiful	uneventful
underwriter	undying	unexaggerated
undeserved	unearned	unexampled
undesigned	unearth	unexcelled
undetermined	unearthly	unexceptionable
undeveloped	uneasy	unexpected
undigested	uneasily	unexpired
undignified	uneasiness	unexplored
undimmed	uneatable	unexpressed
undisciplined	uneaten	unextinguished
undisclosed	uneducated	unfaithful
undisguised	unembarrassed	unfamiliar
undismayed	unemployment	unfashionable
undisposed	unencumbered	unfasten
undisputed	unending	unfavorable
undistinguishable	unendorsed	unfeigned
undisturbed	unendurable	unfinished
undivided	unenforceable	unfold
undo	unenterprising	unforgettable
undone	unenvied	unforgivable
undoubted	unequaled	unfortified
undress	unequivocal	unfortunate
undulate	unerring	unfrequented

unfriendly	unidiomatic	uninvited
unfruitful	uniform	union
unfulfilled	uniformity	unionism
unfurnished	unify	unionist
ungainly	unification	unionize
ungodly	unimaginable	unique
ungovernable	unimaginative	unison
ungracious	unimpaired	unissued
ungrateful	unimpeachable	unit
unguent	unimportant	Unitarian
unhampered	unimpressionable	unitary
unhandy	unindorsed	unite
unhappy	uninfluenced	united
unhardened	uninformed	unity
unharness	uninhabitable	universe
unhealthy	uninhabited	universality
unheard	uninitiated	universally
unhesitating	uninjured	university
unhinge	uninstructed	unjustifiable
unholy	unintelligent	unkind
unhonored	unintelligible	unkindliness
unhook	unintentional	unknightly
unhoped	unintentionally	unknit
unicorn	uninterested	unknown
unidentified	uninterrupted	unknowable

unknowing

unladylike

unlaundered

unlawful

unlearn

unleavened

unless

unlettered

unlicensed

unlike

unlikely

unlisted

unlovable

unlucky

unmailable

unmake

unman

unmanageable

unmannerly

unmarried

unmask

unmerited

unmindful

unmistakable

unmistaken

unmitigated

unmolested

unmounted

unnamed

unnatural

unnecessary

unnerve

unnumbered

unobjectionable

unobservant

unobtainable

unoccupied

unopened

unorganized

unorthodox

unostentatious

unpaid

unpalatable

unparalleled

unpardonable

unparliamentary

unpartisan

unpleasant

unpolished

unpopular

unprecedented

unprejudiced

unpremeditated

unprincipled

unprofessional

unprofitable

unprogressive

unpromising

unpublished

unpunctual

unqualified

unquestionable

unquestioned

unquiet

unreasonable

unrecognized

unredeemed

unrelated

unrepentant

unreproved

unrequired

unresisting

unrestrained

unrestricted

unrivaled

unruled	unsought	untidy
unruly	unsound	untidily
unsafe	unspeakable	until
unsaid	unspecified	unto
unsalable	unspoiled	untold
unsanctified	unspoken	untouched
unsatisfactory	unstained	untoward
unschooled	unstamped	untracked
unscrupulous	unsteadily	untroubled
unseasonable	unstinted	untrue
unseemly	unstrung	untruthful
unseen	unstudied	unusable
unselfish	unsubstantial	unused
unserviceable	unsuccessful	unusual
unsettled	unsuitable	unutterable
unship	unsung	unvarnished
unsightly	unsuspected	unversed
unsigned	unswerving	unwarrantable
unskilled	unsymmetrical	unwarranted
unskillful	unsystematic	unwary
unsociable	untainted	unwashed
unsoiled	untamed	unwavering
unsoldierly	untangle	unwelcome
unsolicited	untarnished	unwell
unsophisticated	unthinkable	unwholesome

unwieldy		uppermost		disuse	
unwilling		upright		misuse	
unwind		uproar		unused	
unwound		upset		usable	
unwise		upstairs		usage	
unwitting		upstart		useful	
unwonted		up-to-date		usefulness	
unworldly		uptown		useless	
unworthy		upward		usher	
unwrap		upholster		usual	
unwreathe		upholsterer		unusual	
unwritten		upholstery		usually	
unyielding		uranium		usury	
up		urban		usufruct	
upbraid		interurban		usurer	
upheaval		suburban		usurious	
upheld		urbane		usurp	
uphill		urbanity		usurpation	
uphold		urge		usurper	
upkeep		urged		utensil	
upland		urgency		utilize	
uplift		urgent		unutilized	
upmost		urn		utilitarian	
upon		use		utilitarianism	
upper		abuse		utility	

utilizable	unutterable	utterly
utmost	utterance	uttermost
utter	uttered	utters

V

vacate
vacancy
vacant
vacation
vacationist
vaccinate
vaccination
vacillate
vacillation
vacuum
vacuity
vacuous
vagabond
vagary
vagrant
vagrancy
vague
vain
vainglory
vainness
vanity
valance
valedictory
valedictorian

valence
valentine
valerian
valet
valiant
valid
invalid
validate
validation
validity
validly
valise
valley
valor
valorous
value
evaluate
invaluable
revaluation
valuable
valuation
valueless
valve
valvular
vampire

vanadium
vanguard
vanilla
vanish
vanity
vanquish
vantage
vapid
vapor
evaporate
vaporization
vaporize
vaporous
varnish
vary
invariable
variability
variable
variance
variant
variation
variegate
variety
various
vassal

vassalage	vendible	verbal
vast	veneer	verbally
vaudeville	venerate	verbatim
vault	venerable	verbiage
vaulted	veneration	verbose
vaunt	vengeance	verbosity
vaunted	vengeful	verbena
vedette	venial	verdict
vegetable	venison	verdigris
vegetarian	venom	verdure
vegetarianism	venomous	verdant
vegetate	ventilate	verge
vegetation	unventilated	verify
vegetative	ventilation	verification
vehement	ventilator	verily
vehemence	ventricle	verisimilitude
vehicle	ventriloquism	veritable
vehicular	venture	veracious
velocipede	venturesome	verity
velocity	venturous	vermilion
velvet	venue	vermin
venal	veracity	vermicide
venality	veracious	vermiform
vend	veranda	vermifuge
vender	verb	verminous

vermuth	vestige	viceregal
vernacular	vestigial	vicinity
vernal	vestment	vicious
vernier	vestry	vicissitudes
versatility	Vesuvian	victim
versatile	veteran	victimize
verse	veterinary	victor
versification	veto	victorious
versify	vex	victory
version	vexation	victual
verso	vexatious	viewed
versus	viaduct	interview
vertebra	vial	purview
vertebrae	viand	review
vertebrate	vibrate	vigil
vertex	vibrancy	vigilance
vertical	vibrant	vigilant
vertigo	vibration	vigor
very	vibrational	vigorous
veriest	vibrator	vile
vesicle	vibratory	vilification
vesper	vicar	vilify
vessel	vicarage	village
vest	vicarious	villager
vestibule	viceroy	villain

villainous	virago	invisible
villainy	virgin	visibility
vindicate	virginal	visible
vindicable	virginity	visionary
vindication	virility	visual
vindicatory	virile	visualization
vindictive	virtue	visualize
vinegar	virtual	visually
vinaigrette	virtually	visit
vineyard	virtuous	revisited
vintage	virtuoso	visitation
viol	virtuosity	visitor
violate	virus	visor
inviolable	virulence	vista
violation	virulent	vital
violative	visa	devitalize
violator	visage	vitality
violence	viscera	vitalization
violent	viscid	vitalize
violet	viscidity	vitally
ultra-violet	viscosity	vitamin
violin	viscous	vitiate
violinist	viscount	vitiated
violoncello	vise	vitiation
viper	vision	vitrify

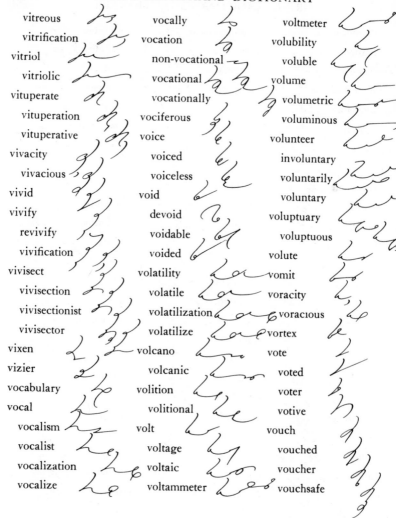

vitreous	vocally	voltmeter
vitrification	vocation	volubility
vitriol	non-vocational	voluble
vitriolic	vocational	volume
vituperate	vocationally	volumetric
vituperation	vociferous	voluminous
vituperative	voice	volunteer
vivacity	voiced	involuntary
vivacious	voiceless	voluntarily
vivid	void	voluntary
vivify	devoid	voluptuary
revivify	voidable	voluptuous
vivification	voided	volute
vivisect	volatility	vomit
vivisection	volatile	voracity
vivisectionist	volatilization	voracious
vivisector	volatilize	vortex
vixen	volcano	vote
vizier	volcanic	voted
vocabulary	volition	voter
vocal	volitional	votive
vocalism	volt	vouch
vocalist	voltage	vouched
vocalization	voltaic	voucher
vocalize	voltammeter	vouchsafe

vowel

voyage

vulcanize

vulcanization

vulgar

vulgarian

vulgarism

vulgarization

vulgarize

vulgarly

Vulgate

vulnerable

invulnerable

vulnerability

vulture

W

wabble		warpath		washer
waddle		warrior		washout
wafer		warship		washstand
waffle		ward		wasp
waft		warden		wassail
wage		wardrobe		waste
wager		warehouse		wastage
Wagnerian		warm		wastebasket
wagon		warmed		wasteful
waist		warmth		wastrel
wakeful		warn		watch
walk		warned		watchcase
walker		warp		watchdog
walkout		warrant		watchful
walnut		unwarrantable		watchmaker
walrus		warranted		watchman
waltz		warrantor		watch tower
wampum		warranty		watchword
wander		warren		water
want		wary		watercourse
unwanted		unwary		waterfall
war		was		waterfowl
warfare		wash		water-logged
warlike		unwashed		watermark
		washable		watermelon

watershed		wealth		well-favored	
water-tight		wealthily		welter	
waterway		weapon		were	
waterworks		weary		west	
watery		wearily		westerly	
watt		wearisome		western	
wattage		weasel		westerner	
wattmeter		weather		westward	
waver		weather-beaten		wet	
unwavering		weathercock		wetness	
wax		weatherproof		whack	
waxed		web		whale	
waxen		week		whaleback	
waxiness		weekday		whalebone	
way		week-end		wharf	
waybill		weekly		wharfage	
wayfarer		weep		wharfinger	
wayside		weight		wharves	
wayward		weird		what	
weak		welcome		somewhat	
weaken		unwelcome		whatever	
weakened		well		whatnot	
weakling		unwell		whatsoever	
weakly		welfare		wheat	
weakness		well-born		wheaten	

wheatworm	while	whither
wheel	whilom	whittle
when	whilst	who
whenever	whim	whoever
whensoever	whimsical	whole
whence	whimsicality	unwholesome
where	whine	whole-hearted
whereabouts	whip	wholesale
whereas	whipcord	wholesaler
whereat	whippet	wholesome
whereby	whipstock	wholly
wherefore	whirl	whoop
wherefrom	whirlpool	whose
wherein	whirlwind	why
whereof	whisk	wicked
whereon	whisky	wickedness
wheresoever	whisper	wickerwork
whereupon	whist	wicket
wherever	whistle	wide
wherewith	white	widen
wherewithal	whitecap	wideness
whether	whitefish	widespread
which	whiten	width
whichever	whiteness	widow
whichsoever	whitewood	widowed

widower		wine		witticism	
widowhood		wineglass		wittily	
wield		wing		wittiness	
unwieldy		wingless		witch	
wife		wink		witchery	
wigwag		winner		with	
wigwam		winter		notwithstanding	
wild		wipe		within	
wilderness		wiper		without	
wildfire		wire		withdraw	
wildness		wireless		withdrawal	
will		wirepulling		withdrawn	
unwilling		wise		withdrew	
willful		unwise		withhold	
willow		wisdom		withheld	
wily		wisely		withstand	
winch		wiser		withstood	
wind		wisest		witness	
wind		wish		wizard	
windage		unwished		wizardry	
windbreak		wisher		woe	
windfall		wishful		woebegone	
windily		wistaria		woeful	
windmill		wit		wolf	
window		unwitting		wolfhound	

wolfish	wood	worker
wolverine	woodcraft	workhouse
wolves	woodcut	workman
woman	wooded	workmanship
unwomanly	wooden	workshop
womanhood	woodland	worktable
womankind	woodman	world
womanlike	woodpecker	unworldly
womanliness	woodsman	worldliness
womanly	woodwork	worldly
women	woodworm	worm
won	woof	hookworm
wonder	wool	worm-eaten
wonderful	woolen	wormhole
wonderland	word	wormwood
wonderment	worded	worry
wonderstricken	wordily	worried
wonderwork	wordiness	worriment
wondrous	wore	worrisome
won't	work	worse
wont	rework	worst
unwonted	unworkable	worship
woo	workable	worshiper
wooed	workaday	worshipful
wooer	worked	worshipped

worsted		wreath		wring	
worth		wreck		wringer	
unworthy		shipwreck		wrinkle	
worthily		wreckage		wrist	
worthiness		wrecker		writ	
worthless		wrench		write	
worthy		wrest		rewrite	
would		wrestle		writer	
wound		wrestler		written	
wounded		wretch		wrong	
wound		wretchedness		wronged	
wove		wriggle		wrongful	
wraith		wright		wrong-headed	
wrangle		millwright		wrongly	
wrath		playwright		wrongness	
wrathful		shipwright		wroth	

X, Y, Z

xebec	
xenon	
xylophone	
yacht	
yachtsman	
yak	
yam	
yank	
yard	
yardage	
yardarm	
yardstick	
yarn	
yawl	
ye	
yea	
year	
yearbook	
yearling	
yearly	
yearn	
yeast	

yell	
yellow	
yeoman	
yeomanry	
yes	
yesterday	
yet	
yield	
unyielding	
yodel	
yolk	
you	
yourself	
young	
younger	
youngest	
youngish	
youngster	
youth	
youthful	
youthfulness	
ytterbium	
yttrium	

yule	
yuletide	
zeal	
zealot	
zealotry	
zealous	
zebra	
zebu	
zenith	
zephyr	
Zeppelin	
zero	
zest	
zigzag	
zinc	
Zion	
zircon	
zirconium	
zither	
zodiac	
zone	
zoölogy	
zwieback